DES/TECH/ED.

GW00467510

Anthropometrics:
an introduction

Stephen Pheasant

'Which of you by taking thought can
add one cubit unto his stature?'

St Matthew vi 27

BSI
Linford Wood, Milton Keynes MK14 6LE
Telephone: 0908 221166

First published 1984 (0 580 13905 0)
PP 7310
UDC 572.087 : 658.512.2
ISBN 0 580 18234 7

Contents

Foreword

In 1984 BSI produced the first edition of this book to provide teachers and students of design with an easy-to-follow introduction to anthropometrics. Designers in a range of disciplines need data about people − their sizes and shapes − to make sure that products fit their users.

Anthropometric data does not stay the same year after year. The characteristics of the population change. We are, in general, becoming a taller people; we are living longer. Such factors change the database.

This second edition of PP 7310 has been revised and extended. The dimensions for British adults have been increased from 50 to 110, the number of worked examples has been increased from three to seven and now include suggestions for project work; and the appendix has been extended to include statistical tables and formulae.

With the advent of a National Curriculum in England and Wales the Design/Technology area has been expanded to include home economics. This book now includes a range of dimensions specifically used by clothing designers so that the application of anthropometrics can be shown throughout the new Design/Technology Curriculum.

This book is an invaluable reference for programmes of study for key stages 2, 3 and 4.

The British Standards cited are those that were current 30 June 1990. Standards are continually under review and revisions and amendments are published frequently. The status of standards may be checked by telephoning BSI's Enquiries Section on 0908 221166.

Derek Prior
Head of Education, BSI

1. Introduction

Ergonomics is the application of scientific information about human beings to the problems of design. If an object, an environment or a system is intended for human use then its design should be based on the characteristics of its human users. Ergonomics is the art and science of matching the product to the user. In North America ergonomics is called 'human factors engineering'. Anthropometrics is the branch of ergonomics which deals with measurements of the physical characteristics of human beings – particularly their sizes and shapes.

Applications for anthropometrics can be found in (almost) all areas of design. All types of furniture, from seating to storage units, will be better suited to their purposes if their dimensions are matched to those of their users. Consumer products, ranging from cooking pots to computer terminals will be more easily, efficiently and safely usable if anthropometric factors are taken into account in their design. Human dimensions are equally important in the design of the environments in which these objects are used – from kitchens and offices to submarines and space vehicles.

In some cases a single critical dimension will be all that is required; other cases may demand the lengthy and complex manipulation of data. Certain basic principles are common to all of these situations – an understanding of which will aid the designer in solving his or her own specific problems. The purpose of this brief text is to explain in plain language these basic principles.

Only under a very few special circumstances is it possible to customize a product for a single user. (Haute couture, motor racing, astronautics and the rehabilitation of the severely disabled are cases in point.) But in most circumstances, it will be necessary to match the product to a population of users who come in a variety of shapes and sizes. We shall call these people the *user population* or the *target population*.

In order that we may succinctly describe the variability of human beings in any particular respect, we shall need to learn some of the mathematical vocabulary of descriptive statistics. But before doing so, certain major heresies must be exposed. These are summarized in the 'five fundamental fallacies' shown in table 1. They are more common than you probably think.

Table 1. The five fundamental fallacies

1   This design is satisfactory for me – it will therefore be satisfactory for everybody else.

2   This design is satisfactory for the average person – it will therefore be satisfactory for everybody else.

3   The variability of people is so great that they cannot possibly be catered for in any design – but since people are wonderfully adaptable it doesn't matter anyway.

4   Ergonomics is expensive and since products are actually purchased on appearance and styling, ergonomic considerations may be conveniently ignored.

5   Ergonomics is an excellent idea. I always design things with ergonomics in mind – but I do it intuitively and rely on my common sense so I don't need experimental studies or tables of data.

Quoted from Pheasant (1986)

First, the designer who matches a product to himself, in the belief that it will be equally suitable for others, will satisfy only those people who are of similar physique and a like mind. How often do you hear a woman condemning a product by saying 'You can tell it was designed by a man'? The problem is that 'placing yourself in another person's shoes' requires an act of imagination of which few of us are capable – however 'intuitive' we may consider ourselves to be. Empirical evidence concerning the remainder of the human race is really much more reliable.

The second major heresy is designing for 'the average man' – or for that matter the 'average person'. Let us take an obvious, albeit somewhat extreme, example. Supposing we were to design a door according to the height and bodily breadth (shoulders, hips, etc.) of the average person. A moment's reflection would show us that 50% of people would have to turn sideways to get through. Since the tallest people are not necessarily the broadest, our design would inconvenience more that half of the user population. Clearly no reasonable person would make such an elementary mistake in designing a door. Nonetheless, equivalent errors are frequently made in designing furniture, and the heresy of the average user remains a popular one (at least among students of ergonomics and design who have imperfectly grasped the principles of anthropometrics).

It is perfectly true that people are adaptable. So they put up with all sorts of deficiencies in the design of the products they use (and they do not necessarily even complain very much). But since people are not infinitely adaptable, bad design may have undesirable long term effects. Conditions such as back pain are commonly caused by the unsatisfactory working postures which result from a failure to consider anthropometric factors in the design of furniture and workstations, etc. People who suffer such afflictions may become acutely aware of ergonomic mismatches which go unnoticed by the rest of us. This makes them very intolerant of bad design.

In applying anthropometric data to any particular design problem, our objective will generally be to provide an *acceptable match* for the greatest possible number of users. Having done so, it may well be advantageous to contrive an *optimum match* for the average person (who as we shall see in due course is the most *probable* user).

2. Statistical aspects

The concepts of descriptive statistics are based on the laws of chance. Supposing you work in a large public building. All sorts of people are wandering in and out for various reasons. It might occur to you to make bets on the height of the next person you meet as you walk down the corridor. It is just possible that your chance encounter would be with a giant or a dwarf — but much more likely that it would be with a man or woman of more or less average stature. (Children are not admitted to your building.) We can immediately see that average people are more *probable* than extreme people — you encounter them more *frequently*. Figure 1

is a graph in which a person's height is plotted on the horizontal axis. The vertical axis denotes the probability of encountering a person of that particular height (or the frequency with which they occur in your target population). Such a presentation of statistical information is called a *probability density function* or a *frequency distribution*.

Figure 1 shows us that the greatest probability (frequency of encounter) is associated with average height and that as you move in either direction from this point encounters become increasingly unlikely (infrequent) in a very systematic way. (Note that the descent from maximum probability does not have a constant gradient.)

Statisticians tend to refer to the average as the *mean*. Since the probability function is symmetrical about this point we can easily see that 50% of the population are taller and 50% are shorter — there is an even chance that your encounter will be with a person of greater than average height. Another name for the average therefore is the fiftieth percentile (50th %le). If all this seems terribly obvious to you, consider whether these statements would be equally true when describing a person's annual income rather than his stature.

In figure 1 there is a certain point on the horizontal axis, somewhere to the left of the average, at which we could say 'only one person in twenty (5% of the population) is shorter than this'. We call this height the 5th percentile. An equal distance to the right of the average is a height which is exceeded by just 5% of the population — this we call the 95th percentile. In general then, n% of the population are smaller (or lighter or weaker) than the nth percentile.

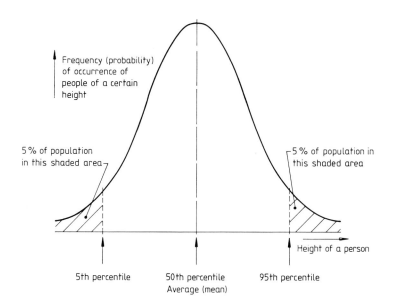

Ninety per cent of the population fall between the 5th and 95th percentiles. Equally, 90% of the population fall between the 9th and 99th percentiles. But the 5th and 95th percentile range is special because it is the shortest distance on the horizontal axis which includes 90% of the population.

The particular probability function we have been discussing, characterized by a symmetrical bell-shaped curve, is called the *normal distribution*. The term 'normal' does not refer to the members of the population — contrasting them for example with 'abnormal' people. It might most appropriately be thought of as meaning 'the distribution which you will find most useful in practical affairs'. Because of this potential confusion, some people prefer to call this distribution 'Gaussian' — after the man who discovered it.

You will find the probability function of the normal distribution tabulated in the appendix.

Any normal distribution can be completely described by two *parameters* — the mean or average *(m)* and the standard deviation *(s)*. The mean locates the centre of the distribution, pinning it down on the horizontal axis. The standard deviation is an index of the degree of variation about this point, i.e. the 'width' of the distribution or the extent to which the various percentiles are spread out along the horizontal axis. We need not know how to define the standard deviation — it is sufficient to know how to use it. A mathematical definition is found in the appendix. Supposing we compare the heights of the adult male population at large with the heights of policemen. On average the policemen are taller; but the degree of variability within the ranks of the police is much less. A statistician would say that the mean height of the police is greater than that of the public and that the standard deviation is smaller.

If we know the mean and standard deviation for a certain distribution, we can calculate the value x_p of any percentile we choose by the equation

$$x_p = m + zs$$

where p is the desired percentile and z is a factor for that particular percentile which we simply look up in a table like table A.2 in the appendix. It so happens that for the 5th and 95th percentiles, $z = -1.64$ and $z = +1.64$ respectively.

In the tables which follow, only the 5th, 50th and 95th percentiles have been given — since these are the ones most commonly used for practical purposes. The standard deviations have also been included so that you may calculate any other percentiles you require.

Most anthropometric characteristics are normally distributed in most user populations — or show deviations from normality which can be ignored for practical purposes. Exceptions include body weight and those circumferences which are strongly dependent on it — such as waist girth, etc. Muscular strength measurements are also in this category. These bodily characteristics have distributions which are asymmetric such that the maximum probability and the 50th percentile are less than the mean — due to the disproportionate presence of very heavy or strong individuals and absence of light or weak ones. Such distributions are said to be *positively skewed*. Furthermore, the combination of two or more normal distributions (such as adults and children, or men and women) does not create a new normal distribution, although the differences between the combination and a true normal distribution will often be small enough to be ignored. Such topics are, however, beyond the scope of this text and the interested reader should consult one of the more advanced volumes in the bibliography.

Deviations from normality are only important insomuch as they lead to errors in the calculation of percentiles. In many cases an *ad hoc* correction to the calculated percentile should suffice. Suggestions concerning the magnitude of such corrections are given in the notes to the anthropometric data in section 4.

People differ not only in size but also in shape. So in some design problems it is necessary to consider not only the variability in the relevant body dimensions — but also the relationships between them. In order to do this, we need to know about another statistical parameter — the correlation coefficient, which is usually designated by the letter r. (You will find it defined in the appendix.) Two variables which have a perfect, linear, one-to-one relationship with each other, are said to have a correlation of $r = 1$. (Measurements of dimensions such as shoulder height, taken on the right and left sides of the body, would have a correlation of very nearly 1 — the actual figure is about 0.99, since we are not quite symmetrical.) Two variables which are not related at all, are said to have a correlation of $r = 0$. (Stature and annual salary would have a correlation of almost zero.) The dimensions used in anthropometrics rarely approach either of these extremes.

Body dimensions fall into certain fairly obvious categories — limb lengths (together with the heights above the ground of various parts of the anatomy), trunk breadths, trunk and limb circumferences, etc. In general we would expect the members of any particular categories to be relatively well-correlated with each other — but relatively poorly with the members of other categories. Hence lengths correlate well with other lengths — but poorly with circumferences. We would also expect members of a particular category which involve closely related landmarks to have a higher correlation than those which involve distantly related ones. Hence eye height has a better correlation with stature than knee height.

The correlation coefficient is very important in the anthropometrics of clothing design — because it enables us to do things like calculating the range of sleeve lengths to provide for in a given collar size (see 7.7). Details of how to perform these calculations (together with certain other important uses for the correlation coefficient) are given in the appendix.

3. Using anthropometric data

In this section we shall consider a systematic approach to practical anthropometrics, which is known as the *method of limits*. It involves searching for the boundary conditions which would make an object 'too large', 'too small' or 'just right'. It has a wide applicability in furniture design, product design, environmental design, etc. The anthropometric problems involved in clothing design are somewhat specialized and will be dealt with separately.

3.1 Choice of criteria

Anthropometrics deals with the relationships between the dimensions of the user and those of the object. These relationships are of three basic kinds:

(i) Clearance;
(ii) Reach;
(iii) Posture.

Clearance (head room, knee room, elbow room, etc.) must be adequate to accommodate the bodily dimensions of a large-sized member of the user population. In these cases, anthropometric data allow us to specify the minimum dimension acceptable in the object. Hence the height of a table (underside) should not be less than the knee height of a 95th percentile user.

Reach dimensions, on the other hand, should be based on a small member of the population. They allow us to specify the maximum dimension allowable in the object. Hence the height of a seat should not be greater than the lower leg length of a 5th percentile user. (This particular dimension is usually called popliteal height since anatomists call the back of the knee the popliteal region.)

Consider the implications of these statements. A clearance which is adequate for the 95th percentile user will (by definition) also be satisfactory for the 95% of the user population who are smaller. Similarly, a reach which is within the capacity of the 5th percentile user will also be within the capacity of the 95% of the population who are larger. We may say that these percentages of the user population have been *accommodated* with respect to the relevant *anthropometric criterion*. (An anthropometric criterion is an operationally clear statement of what constitutes an acceptable relationship between the dimensions of the person and those of the object he is using.) In both cases we may satisfy the majority by designing for the *limiting user* − a hypothetical individual in whichever tail of the distribution it is, that imposes the most severe constraint on the design. (Contrast this with design for the average man.) Bear in mind that both clearance and reach dimensions impose a constraint *in one direction only* − we call them *one-tailed constraints*.

In the examples given above, the criteria do not tell us when the table is too high or the chair is too low − in order to determine these limits you must look elsewhere. Note also that if you wish to actively prevent access, or to place an object out of reach (in the interests of safety for example), then the usual criteria will be reversed (see 6.5).

In another very important class of problems, the relationship between the dimensions of people and workspaces determines, for better or worse, the working posture of the operator. Postural problems are often more complicated than those of clearance and reach. Supposing we wish to determine the optimum height of a kitchen worktop. It is not self-evident that we should design either for tall or short people particularly. Various studies have shown that such a worktop should be between 50 mm and 100 mm below the elbow height of the user when standing. On the basis of this criterion we could select the worktop height which 'accommodates' the greatest possible proportion of the target population. (It is in fact 75 mm below the elbow height of the average user − can you work out why?) If the height which is chosen falls outside the desirable limits for a significant proportion of the population, we have to decide whether the problems arising from a worktop which is too high are worse than those arising from one which is too low or vice versa. Such a consideration might lead us to shift our determined height upward or downward in order to achieve the best possible compromise. Or it might lead us to conclude that an adjustable worktop was required.

Many problems of postural relationship are best solved by the provision of adjustable equipment; office chairs are an obvious example. The adjustment should allow a broad range of the population (e.g. from the 5th to 95th percentiles) to work in a satisfactory position. We must bear in mind that the success of our design depends not only on obtaining appropriate anthropometric data, and using it appropriately, but also on the quality of our criteria. If we cannot establish a clear operational definition of what constitutes a good posture for a certain task our design solutions will at best be tentative.

The desirability of accommodating a broad spectrum of the user population should by now be clear. But why should we choose particular percentiles such as the 5th and 95th? There is no hard and fast answer to a question of this kind. Because of the shape of the normal curve, it is increasingly difficult to accommodate extreme percentiles of the population. Consider where the various percentile points must fall on the horizontal axis of figure 1. They are densely packed in the centre and thinly spread in the tails. Thinking in cost/benefit terms, each additional per cent of the population accommodated imposes a more severe design constraint. So as we enter the tails of the distribution we are in a situation of rapidly diminishing returns. The 5th and 95th percentiles are

purely arbitrary cut-off points which designers have found convenient in a wide range of applications.

These cut-off points are called the *design limits*. The more severe the consequences of a mismatch, the wider we should set the design limits. In the case of a safety clearance (for example), it might be appropriate to set our cut-off at a value of 3 or 3.5 standard deviations above the mean. In theory, the former could still leave about one user in 1000 at risk − the latter perhaps one user in 10,000.

3.2 Static and dynamic data

Distinctions are often drawn between static (or structural) anthropometrics and dynamic (or functional) anthropometrics. The difference may be illustrated by comparing the length of a person's arm from the shoulder to the fingertip with the distance he can reach in a certain direction, to grasp a certain kind of handle, while seated in a certain way. The former gives general (perhaps rough) guidance in a broad range of situations; the latter may well be specific to a single application. Most of the data presented here are of the former kind. Dynamic data must, in general, be gathered as the situation arises. (Note that the terms 'static' and 'dynamic' do not necessarily imply the absence or presence of movement.)

3.3 Fitting trials and mock-ups

The creative use of anthropometric data will suffice to solve many problems − and the principal emphasis of this text will be in this direction. But there will always be occasions on which there is no substitute for trial and error. In these cases it may be appropriate to perform a *fitting trial* − an experimental study in which the designer systematically explores user preferences, by means of an adjustable mock-up of the product concerned. (See 7.6 for an example.) Mock-ups need not be elaborate — a great deal can be achieved using plywood off-cuts and cardboard boxes — it is largely a matter of ingenuity. The advantage of this approach is that it is almost entirely empirical and makes relatively few assumptions concerning criteria, etc. (The validity of these assumptions may be questionable.) And if we rely too exclusively on pencil and paper methods we may overlook certain aspects of the problem. The principal disadvantages of the fitting trial approach are that formal controlled experimentation is laborious and representative samples of users can be difficult to find. It is not always easy to know where you can cut corners in these respects, without defeating the purpose of the study.

There are no rules for deciding between the pencil-and-paper approach to anthropometrics and the fitting trial. It is to some extent a matter of judgement and to some extent a matter of the way that you personally prefer to work. But it is always a good idea to try out your design on a representative sample of users — preferably at a sufficiently early stage in the project, before you have reached the point when modifications are no longer practicable.

3.4 Standard postures

Most anthropometric measurements are made in one of two standardized postures — the standing and the sitting. The standard standing position is fully erect with the feet together and the eyes looking directly forward. See figure 3(a). The standard sitting position is shown in figure 3(b). The trunk and head are fully erect; the shoulders are relaxed, so that the upper arm hangs vertically; the forearm is horizontal, hence the elbow is at a right angle.

The height of the seat is adjusted (or supports are placed beneath the feet) until the thighs are horizontal, the lower legs are vertical and the feet are flat on the floor — hence the knee and ankle joints are also at right angles. Vertical measurements such as 'sitting eye

height' will always be given from the seat surface unless clearly specified otherwise. Horizontal measurements (see figure 3(c)) are made from a vertical reference plane which touches the uncompressed buttocks and/or the shoulders. (In some measurement techniques this plane is real, e.g. a wall; in others it is imaginary.) The intersection between the vertical reference plane and the seat surface is known as the seat reference point (SRP).

Extrapolating from the standard postures in which measurements have been made to other situations calls for a certain amount of ingenuity and a degree of informed guesswork.

3.5 Clothing corrections

Anthropometrics measurements are usually made on people who are unshod and minimally clad. The data in the tables which follow all refer to people without clothes or shoes. Since most (but not all) environments are designed for clothed users, appropriate corrections must be made. The most important is to add, where appropriate, a correction for the heels of shoes. Heels may range in height from 10 mm for carpet slippers to 125 mm or even 150 mm for the most extreme varieties of women's fashion shoes. (At the time of writing, fashions are less extreme.) We need therefore to estimate, in each specific situation, what the average heel height of our target population is likely to be. It is quite adequate to add the same increment to all the percentiles, since the variability in heel height will always be small compared with anthropometric variability.

Most products will continue in use throughout several of the periodic fluctuations of fashion in footwear. We cannot therefore identify a single 'correct' increment for heel height. Taking one consideration with another the following corrections seem appropriate for outdoor or semi-formal situations (offices, public buildings, etc.):

Add 25 mm for men or 45 mm for women to all dimensions which include the heel of the shoe. (Assume that all children under 12 and boys above this age wear 25 mm heels — and that girls over 12 wear 45 mm heels.)

Other clothing corrections may be estimated as the situation demands. Will the equipment user be wearing indoor or outdoor clothes? Will he be wearing a hat? Ask yourself these questions and make estimates of the corrections you require. Indoor clothing can usually be ignored. Heavy outdoor clothing may add up to 40 mm to clearances.

3.6 User populations

Accurate anthropometric calculations require reliable data for the relevant user populations. To get such data we need to make careful measurements of large numbers of people. (Between 500 and 1000 individuals should suffice, provided they are a representative sample.) Anthropometric surveys are costly and time consuming and few organizations (other than the armed services) have the time and resources to perform them. Most of us therefore have to muddle through with data of a distinctly patchy kind.

The principal factors affecting the anthropometrics of a population are age, sex, ethnicity, and occupation. Within a national sample there may also be regional and social class differences. These matters are discussed at length in Pheasant (1986) — a brief summary will be given here.

The two factors which are most likely to be of importance to the designer are sex and age. The anatomical differences between men and women are too well known to require elaboration. Full adult stature is attained at around 18 years in boys and a little earlier in girls. Body breadths (e.g. across the shoulders) continue

to increase until the mid-twenties whereas body weight and related dimensions may increase throughout life. Cross-sectional studies, in which the dimensions of adults of various ages have been recorded, generally show a steady decline in stature from youth to old age. Some people literally shrink with age — due to changes in the form and function of the spine. Probably more important is the fact that each new generation is a little taller than its predecessor. This upward trend is believed to have come to a halt in Europe and North America. Elsewhere it may still be occurring. In Japan it is happening rapidly but showing some signs of decline. In India it is possibly working in reverse.

The importance of ethnic minorities in a user population is commonly overestimated. At present about 5% of people living in Britain are of non-European descent. In the USA the figure is around 10%. These percentages are not large enough to make much difference in our calculations. Ethnic differences may, however, be important in the design of goods for export. Contrary to popular belief the adult populations of Britain and the USA are anthropometrically remarkably similar. Differences between European countries are also relatively small — although there are exceptions. But Far Eastern populations (particularly the Japanese) are anthropometrically very different from Europeans.

Some military samples are similar to the civilian populations from which they were selected; others (particularly flying personnel, who are probably the world's most measured group) are substantially different.

3.7 Units and accuracy

How accurate do we need to be when performing anthropometric calculations? The data in this book are all given in millimetres. Most of the data are corrected to the nearest 5 millimetres. This represents the limit of resolution we could require for most practical purposes — even if we had perfect data, which we do not.

Our forefathers used units of measurement derived from the human body — the yard (36 inches) was said to be the length of the arm (measured from breast bone to fingertip), the 'foot' was the length of the human foot and the inch was the breadth of the thumb. There were also some other less well known units — such as the cubit, which was half a yard or the length of the forearm (from elbow to fingertip) and the hand (still used in measuring horses), which was the breadth of the palm or four inches.

Actually an inch (25.4 mm) is the size of a rather large thumb (almost 95th percentile) and feet which are 12 inches long are very rare indeed — you may care to compare the other units with the data in table 2.

In many respects, the inch would be a very good unit to adopt in anthropometrics — since for many practical purposes a tolerance of 25 mm would be acceptable (and the best you can realistically hope for). You might care to think of this as 'the anthropometric inch'.

The data given here are the best estimates available at the present time — but their accuracy cannot be guaranteed. (Nobody has yet had the resources to conduct a sufficiently detailed survey of British adults.) In critical applications, or cases where a closer tolerance is required, the designer must treat these (or any other) data with circumspection. Experience suggests that inaccuracies in anthropometric data, as such, are generally small compared with the margins for error of the criteria we apply. Anthropometrics is rarely (if ever) an exact science.

3.8 Dimensional co-ordination

The system of modular co-ordination, which is used extensively in building design and the standardization of building components, is described in BS 6750 (and in a technically equivalent series of International Standards). It applies not only to the structural components of buildings but also to the spaces these define and the products that fit into them — its purpose being to maximize the dimensional compatibility of the various elements involved. Modular co-ordination and anthropometrics deal with closely related issues, so it is worthwhile considering how the two systems fit together

The system of modular co-ordination is based on an *international basic module* of 100 mm, which is denoted by the symbol M. The co-ordinating dimensions of products or spaces should wherever possible be multiples of M, or preferably 3M. Preferred subdivisions of M are M/2 (first preference) and M/4 (second preference). So the smallest member of this series of preferred sizes is 25 mm of 'the anthropometric inch'. In most cases it will be acceptable to round off the results of anthropometric calculations to the nearest preferred number — clearances should be rounded up and reaches rounded down. There is little cause for the goals of dimensional co-ordination and ergonomics to be incompatible — provided that the dimensions of products and spaces are not chosen by reference to an arbitrary system of preferences rather than by consideration of the human user.

3.9 The problem-solving process

We are now in a position to summarize the thought processes you are likely to go through in applying anthropometric principles to a design problem — and the decision-making steps which are likely to be required. These are shown in the form of a chart in figure 2. In section 7 we shall see some examples of how to make such decisions in practice.

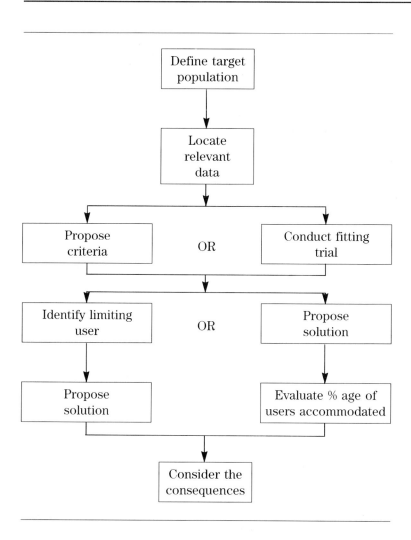

Figure 2. Chart for decision-making steps

4. Definitions of anthropometric dimensions with some comments concerning their applications

The dimensions given in the tables in section 5 will now be defined. They are shown in figure 3. Brief comments concerning their applications are included here together with recommendations for correction factors where these might be required. A further discussion of applications is to be found in section 6. Common English names for bodily dimensions have been used wherever possible with their more precise anatomical equivalents placed in brackets. The term 'popliteal' is used in dimensions 14, 16 and their derivatives since it lacks a suitable English equivalent.

The dimensions tabulated (110 in all) have been divided into nine groups. The first six groups (dimensions 1 to 65) are relevant to a broad range of design applications. The remainder (dimensions 66 to 110) are principally relevant to clothing design.

Notes.
(i)   For some purposes it may be necessary to add two dimensions together, or to calculate their differences − to do this accurately use the equations given in A.5 in the appendix. Some commonly used combinations are given in the tables (dimensions 59 to 65).
(ii)   Suggested clothing and shoe corrections are given in 3.5.

Group A Heights of principal anatomical landmarks

Measured in the standard standing position. Principally used in workstation design and environmental design. Corrections for shoes will generally be required − see 3.5. (For heights of subsidiary landmarks see dimensions 91 to 97.)

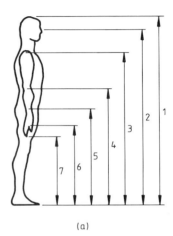

(a)

1 Stature The height of the fully erect standing person. Clearance from floor to overhead obstacles. Stature is an important reference dimension for comparing populations, in anthropometric estimation procedures and for choosing subjects for fitting trials. The length of the recumbent human body is around 25 mm greater than stature. (Note that when subjects are asked their stature they usually over-estimate it by as much as 25 mm. This effect is independent of age and sex.)

2 Eye height The eye level of the standing person. Defines the centre of the visual field and hence is an important reference level for the location and design of visual displays (see 6.2). Also a 'reach' dimension for seeing over visual obstructions.

3 Shoulder height (Acromial) The height of the acromion, i.e. the bony 'point' of the shoulder. It approximately defines the centre of rotation of the shoulder joint; hence it may be used, in conjunction with dimensions 18 and 23, for calculating zones of *reach* (see 6.4). Upper limit for the location of frequently used controls.

4 Elbow height Reference level for determining the heights of working surfaces (see 6.4).

5 Hip height (Trochanteric) Height of the greater trochanter (a bony prominence at the top of the thigh bone). Defines the centre of rotation of the hip joint, and hence the functional length of the lower limb. The level at which loads are commonly carried.

6 Knuckle height Reference level for hand grips. For support (handrails, etc.), a level some 100 mm above knuckle height is desirable. Handholds on objects for carrying should be at less than knuckle height. Lowest acceptable level for most types of hand operated controls. Optimum height for lifting actions (an average value of 750 mm is often quoted).

7 Fingertip height Lowest acceptable height for fingertip operated controls.

Group B Sitting dimensions

Measurements made in the standard sitting position; principally relevant to the design of seating and seated workstations.

Note. Dimensions 8 to 12 are measured from the seat surface. In some cases it might be necessary to make an allowance for seat compression. If heights above the floor are required, *either* add a fixed amount for a non-adjustable seat (e.g. 400 mm); *or*, for an adjustable seat, add popliteal height, using equations 12 and 13 from the appendix.

8 Sitting height Vertical distance of the crown of the head above the seat surface. *Clearance* from seat to overhead obstacles for sitting person. Add 10 mm for thick clothing beneath buttocks,

25 mm for hat, 35 mm for safety helment.

9 Sitting eye height Eye level of the sitting person above the seat surface. Reference level for the location of visual displays (see dimension 2 and 6.2). Subtract up to 40 mm for sitting slump.

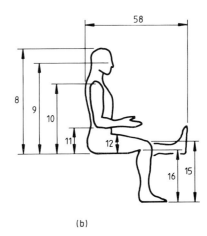

(b)

10 Sitting shoulder height (Acromial) Shoulder level of the sitting person above the seat surface. Subtract up to 40 mm for sitting slump. Used in conjunction with dimensions 18 and 25 for calculating zones of *reach* (see dimension 3).

11 Sitting elbow height The height of the underside of the elbow above the seat. Suitable height for armrests in many seats. Reference level for table heights, etc; keyboards should be at elbow height (but see also dimension 12); writing surfaces should be 50 mm to 100 mm above elbow height.

12 Thigh thickness Vertical distance from the seat surface to the higher part of the thigh. *Clearance* required between seat and underside of table or other obstacle. This dimension interacts strongly with elbow rest height. Typists (for example) generally prefer to raise their seat so as to be 'on top of their work', i.e., the keyboard is a little below the level of the elbow and the shoulders are relaxed. The typist may be prevented from achieving this satisfactory working posture by the need to accommodate her thighs beneath the table. She may therefore be forced to 'perch' uncomfortably on the front edge of her seat (this is a common cause of back pain). The distance between the top of the thigh and the underside of the elbow (combination dimension 61) is not very great. The thickness of table plus keyboard must be accommodated within this distance. Obstacles such as knee-hole drawers are highly undesirable for this reason (see 7.1).

13 Buttock-knee length Horizontal distance from the back of the uncompressed buttocks to the front of the knee in the standard sitting position. *Clearance* required between seat back and obstacles in front of the knee. Add correction for outdoor clothing.

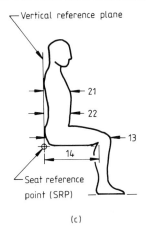

(c)

14 Buttock-popliteal length Horizontal distance from the uncompressed buttocks to the popliteal fossa (i.e. the back of the

knee) in the standard sitting position. Maximum acceptable depth (i.e. front to back dimension) of a seat.

15 Knee height Height of the top of the knee from the floor in the standard sitting position. *Clearance* required beneath tables, etc. Add correction for shoes.

16 Popliteal height Height of the popliteal fossa (i.e. the back of the knee) from the floor in the standard sitting position. Defines the maximum acceptable height of a seat. The optimum height of a seat is commonly quoted as 25 mm to 50 mm below popliteal height. Add correction for shoes.

17 Shoulder breadth (Bideltoid) Maximum breadth across the shoulders. *Clearance* required in upper part of work space. (See also dimension 56.) Add correction for outdoor clothing.

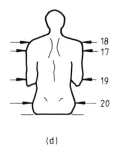

(d)

18 Biacromial breadth Horizontal distance between the acromia (i.e. the bony 'points' of the shoulders). Defines centre of rotation of upper limb (see dimension 3).

19 Elbow-elbow breadth Maximum lateral distance across the elbows while the arms hang loosely by the sides. *Clearance* required at elbow height. (See also dimension 56.) Add correction for outdoor clothing.

20 Hip breadth Maximum lateral distance across the hips. *Clearance* required at seat height (e.g. between the arms of chairs). A very obese person may have a hip breadth of 550 mm. Add correction for outdoor clothing. The breadth of a seat which does not have arms, may comfortably be 50 mm less than hip breadth.

21 Chest (bust) depth Horizontal distance between the back of the shoulder blades and the most prominent part of the chest (or bust in women). *Clearance* required between seat back and obstacles located at above elbow height. Add correction for outdoor clothing. See also dimension 57.

22 Abdominal depth Horizontal distance between the uncompressed buttocks and the most prominent part of the abdomen, in the standard sitting position. *Clearance* required between seat back and obstacles such as table edge, steering wheels, etc. Add correction for outdoor clothing. Abdominal depth, measured in the standing position, is about 25 mm less. A very obese person, or a woman in the later stages of pregnancy, may have an abdominal depth of 450 mm.

Group C Upper limb measurements and reaches

Notes. For a full grasping action subtract 60% of hand length (or 110 mm) from all dimensions measured to the fingertips (i.e. dimensions 23, 25, 26, 28, 29 and 30). For actions involving a pinchgrip (as in operating a rotary knob) subtract 40% of hand length (or 75mm). Dimensions 28 to 30 are 'easy reaches' made without stretching.

23 Shoulder-fingertip length Distance from the acromion to the tip of the middle finger. Defines the radius of the arc of rotation of the upper limb. Used in conjunction with dimensions 3, 10 and 18 for calculating zones of reach.

24 Shoulder-elbow length Distance from the acromion to the

underside of the elbow in the standard sitting position.

25 Elbow-fingertip length Overall distance from the back of the elbow to the tip of the middle finger when the forearm and hand are held horizontally. Reference dimension for the horizontal location of controls.

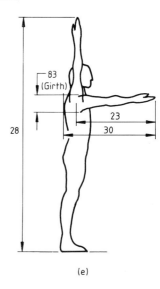

(e)

26 Span Lateral distance between the fingertips when both arms are stretched out sideways. Defines the lateral limits of convenient reach. (In classical times this dimension was considered to be equal to stature in a 'well proportioned' man; hence Leonardo's famous drawing based on the writings of the Roman architect Vitruvius. The span 'defined' a unit of measurement, the fathom, half of which was the yard − see 3.7.)

27 Elbow span Lateral distance between the elbows when both arms are stretched out sideways. A useful dimension when considering 'elbow room' in the workspace.

28 Standing overhead reach Height of middle fingertip above the floor when the arm is raised comfortably above the head without stretching. Overhead limit for location of fingertip operated controls. Add correction for shoes. Add 75 mm for stretching and another 75 mm for standing on tiptoe.

29 Sitting overhead reach Height of middle fingertip above seat surface, when the arm is raised comfortably above the head without stretching. Overhead limit for fingertip operated controls. Add 75 mm for stretching.

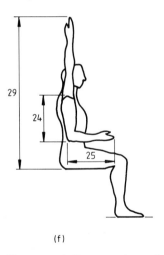

(f)

30 Forward reach Horizontal distance from the back of the shoulder blades to the middle fingertip of the horizontal, forward-reaching, upper limb. (The subject merely raises his arm; he does not thrust his shoulders forward or incline his trunk.) Forward limit for convenient operation of controls. Add 100 mm for a forward thrusting action of the shoulders and another 150 mm for

a 30° inclination of the trunk.

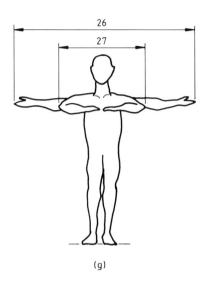

(g)

Group D Hand dimensions
Note. For girths see dimensions 87 to 90.

31 Hand length From the crease of the wrist to the tip of the middle finger.

32 Hand breadth (metacarpal) Overall breadth of the palm at its widest point, i.e. excluding thumb. *Clearance* required for handgrips, etc. By deliberately contracting the palm, this dimension may be reduced by up to 25 mm.

33 Hand breadth (including thumb) As above but with thumb. *Clearance* required for hand access.

34 Palm length From the crease of the wrist to the base of the middle finger.

35 Index finger length From the web to the fingertip. The middle finger is longer (by about 10 mm); the ring finger is about the same length; the little finger is shorter (by about 17 mm).

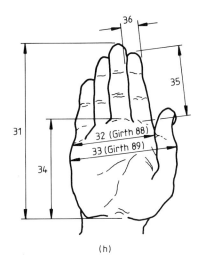

(h)

36 Index finger breadth Across the proximal interphalangeal joint (i.e. the finger joint nearest to the palm). *Clearance* required for fingertip access.

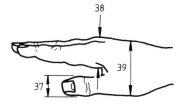

(i)

37 Thumb breadth Across the joint.

38 Hand thickness (at palm) Measured at the thickest point, i.e. across the knuckles but excluding thumb. *Clearance* required in handgrips, etc.

39 Hand thickness (including thumb) As above but also with thumb. *Clearance* required for hand access.

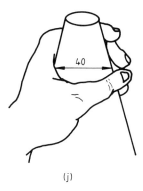

(j)

40 Maximum grip diameter Measured as shown in figure (j).

Group E Foot dimensions

Used in the design of pedals and footwear. (For girths see dimensions 80 to 82.)

41 Foot length From heel to toe. *Clearance* for foot, etc. Add about 30 mm for shoes and 40 mm for boots. Used in the Mondopoint system of shoe sizing (BS 4981, etc.).

42 Foot breadth Overall breadth across the widest point. *Clearance dimension.* Add about 10 mm for shoes and 30 mm for boots. Used in the Mondopoint system of shoe sizing (BS 4981).

43 Heel-ball length Distance from the back of the heel to the head of the first metatarsal, i.e. the 'ball' of the foot. Functional length of the foot in pedal operation.

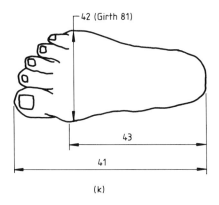

(k)

44 Ankle height Height of the lateral malleolus (a bony prominence on the outside of the ankle) from the ground. Defines the centre of rotation of the foot at the ankle joint. Add correction for shoes.

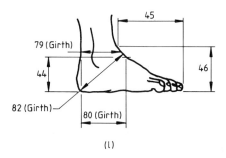

(l)

45 Forefoot length Distance from the toes to the point where the shin meets the top of the foot. *Clearance* dimension for toe recesses, etc. Add about 30 mm for shoes and 40 mm for boots.

46 Instep height Measured to the point where shin meets the top of the foot. *Clearance* dimension for toe recesses. Add correction for shoes.

Group F   Head dimensions

Used in the design of headgear and related products. (For girths see dimensions 66 to 68.)

47 Head length Overall dimension from glabella (a point on the forehead between the two brow ridges) to the occiput (back of the head). The eyes are approximately 20 mm behind the glabella.

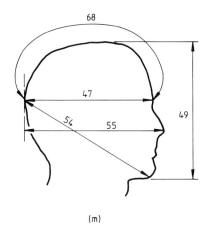

(m)

48 Head breadth Maximum side-to-side dimension of head (excluding ears).

49 Head height Vertical distance from chin to vertex (the highest point of the crown of the head).

50 Ear to crown Vertical distance from the tragus (the flap of cartilage which covers the ear hole) to the vertex.

51 Mouth to crown Vertical distance.

52 Ear to ear breadth As for dimension 48, but including ears.

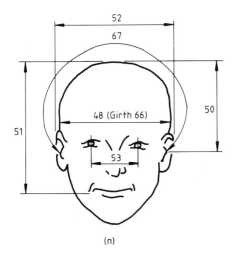

(n)

53 Inter-pupillary breadth Horizontal distance between the pupils of the two eyes.

54 Maximum head diameter From the chin to the most distant point on the back of the head.

55 Nose to back of head Overall horizontal distance.

Group G Additional clearances and combination dimensions

56 Maximum body breadth Overall measurement, made on a standing person, wherever breadth is greatest. Add correction for outdoor clothing.

57 Maximum body depth Overall measurement, made on a standing person, between whatever parts of the body extend the furthest forward and backward respectively. Add correction for outdoor clothing.

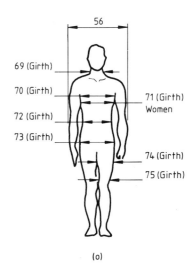

(o)

58 Buttock-heel length From rear of buttocks to soles of feet, with legs stretched out.

The following combination dimensions were calculated using the formulae given in A.5 in the appendix.

59 Popliteal height plus thigh thickness (16+12) *Clearance* under table top.

60 Popliteal height plus elbow height (16+11) Reference dimension for determining table heights.

61 Sitting elbow height minus thigh thickness (11−12)

Clearance between underside of elbows and tops of thighs.

62 Sitting eye height minus elbow height (9−11) Reference dimension for the location of visual displays in relation to keyboards, etc.

63 Elbow-fingertip length minus head length (25−47) Reference dimension for location of visual displays in relation to keyboards, etc.

64 Forward reach minus abdominal depth (30−22) Comfortable reach over an obstacle (see notes to Group C dimensions).

65 Buttock-knee length plus forefoot length (13+45) *Clearance* in seated workspaces at floor level.

Group H Body girths

Except where otherwise stated these are horizontal circumferences measured in a relaxed standing position. Mainly used in clothing design. *Control measurements* for garment sizing (as specified in BS 5511, ISO 3635, etc.) are indicated thus: ● (for further discussion see 6.6).

● **66 Head girth** Maximum circumference above the ears.

67 Coronal arc Measured from ear to ear across the crown of the head.

68 Sagittal arc Measured from glabella to occiput (see dimension 47) across the crown of the head.

● **69 Neck girth** Maximum circumference around the lower part of the neck − just below the laryngeal prominence (Adam's apple) at the level of the seventh cervical vertebra (a bony prominence at the back of the neck).

● **70 Chest (bust) girth** In men at the level of the nipples; in women at the bustpoints (i.e. tips of bra). Measured during normal breathing − increases during deep breathing (50 mm to 75 mm).

● **71 Underbust girth** Immediately below the breasts.

● **72 Waist girth** At the level of the natural waistline (between the hip bones and the ribs) with the subject standing with the muscles relaxed and breathing normally. Increases with deep abdominal breathing (about 50 mm) and on sitting down (about 25 mm).

● **73 Hip girth** Maximum circumference around buttocks (at level of trochanters − see dimension 5).

74 Thigh girth Around the top of the thigh, immediately below the gluteal fold (crease of the buttocks).

75 Lower thigh girth Just above the knee.

76 Knee girth Around the mid-point of the patella (knee cap).

77 Knee girth flexed Around knee cap and popliteal angle, with the knee fully flexed.

78 Calf girth Maximum circumference.

79 Ankle girth Minimum circumference just above the ankle bones.

80 Lower ankle girth Around the bony prominences of the ankle (medial and lateral malleoli).

81 Foot girth (ball) Maximum circumference of the ball of the foot.

82 Foot girth (heel-instep) Around the heel and over the arch of the foot.

83 Scye girth Vertical circumference over the acromion (bony point of the shoulder) and under the armpit. *Scye* is a tailoring term, denoting the armhole of a garment.

84 Biceps girth Maximum circumference of upper arm as it hangs by the side with the muscles relaxed. Flexing muscles increases it by 25 mm (average).

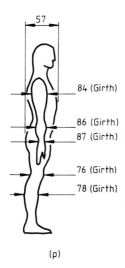

(p)

85 Elbow girth Over the olecranon (bony prominence of the elbow) and around the crotch of the elbow, when it is fully flexed.

86 Forearm girth Maximum circumference of the forearm with the muscles relaxed.

87 Wrist girth Around narrowest point.

88 Hand girth (palm) Around palm at knuckles.

89 Hand girth (including thumb) As dimension 88 with thumb.

90 Fist girth maximum Circumference of fully clenched fist.

Group I Miscellaneous dimensions

Mainly used in clothing design.

91 Cervical height The height of the *vertebra prominens* (seventh cervical vertebra) − palpable at the base of the back of the neck.

92 Axilla height The height of the axillary folds (i.e. the fleshy folds of the armpit).

93 Sternale height The height of the sternal notch (i.e. the top of the breastbone, at the base of the throat).

94 Chest (bust) height In men the height of the nipple; in women the height of the bustpoint (i.e. tip of bra).

95 Waist height The height of the natural waistline (between the hip bones and the ribs). Approximately equal to the tailoring measurement *outside leg* (● − a control dimension for garment sizing).

96 Crotch height Measured from the floor to the crotch with the legs slightly parted. Approximately equal to the tailoring measurement *inside leg* (● − a control dimension for garment sizing).

97 Gluteal height The height of the gluteal fold (i.e. crease of the buttock).

98 Interscye Surface distance across the back between the posterior axillary folds (i.e. the fleshy folds of the armpits).

99 Chest breadth At the level of the nipple.

100 Waist breadth At the natural waistline (between the hip bones and the ribs).

101 Bust breadth Horizontal distance between the bustpoints (i.e. tips of bra).

102 Strap length From bustpoint to bustpoint, passing around the back of the neck at cervical, (see dimension 91).

103 Shoulder length Surface distance from the acromion (bony part of the shoulder) to the junction between the shoulder and the neck.

104 Shoulder angle Subtended by the horizontal and a line drawn from the acromion to the junction between the shoulder and the neck.

105 Sleeve length From the spine to the wrist, measured with the arm raised to the horizontal and the elbow flexed to 90°.

106 Sleeve inseam Measured from the anterior axillary fold (fleshy fold of the armpit) to the wrist.

107 Waist front Surface distance from waist level to sternale (see dimension 93).

108 Waist back Surface distance from waist level to cervical (see dimension 91).

109 Crotch length Surface distance measured under the crotch, from the waistline at front to the waistline at back.

110 Vertical trunk circumference Surface distance measured from the mid-shoulder, down over the nipple (or bustpoint), under the crotch, up over the buttock protrusion and back to the shoulder again.

5. Anthropometric data

5.1 Adults (tables 2 and 3)

The stature and body weight data given in table 2 are taken from a survey of a large and representative sample of British adults, conducted by the Office of Population Censuses and Surveys (Knight 1984). The other dimensions have either been compiled from surveys which match the OPCS sample for height and weight; or estimated using a method of scaling, described in Pheasant (1986). The male data for dimensions 69, 70, 72 to 75, 78, 87 and 109 are quoted from WIRA (1980) and most of the hand data from Kember *et al* (1981). The standing and sitting dimensions, the reaches, the head and the foot dimensions are all estimates, quoted from Pheasant (1986). Other sources used include Kemsley (1957), Damon *et al* (1966), Gooderson and Beebee (1976), NASA (1978) and Haslegrave and Hardy (1979). (These were scaled up or down whenever it seemed appropriate.)

Table 3 is based on a survey of elderly people conducted by the Institute for Consumer Ergonomics at the University of Technology, Loughborough (ICE 1983). Subjects were inmates of geriatric institutions, so they are a fairly extreme sample. Some dimensions are quoted directly from the original; others are estimates taken from Pheasant (1986).

The data given in tables 2 and 3 are the best available at the time of writing. They should not however be seen as definitive — rather, they are a provisional set of figures to be used until further information is available.

Note. Body circumferences (dimensions 66 to 90) are commonly found to have a skewed distribution (see section 2). But the percentiles in table 2 have been calculated on the assumption that they are normally distributed.
It is possible therefore, that the 5th and 95th percentiles are underestimated — but it is not known by how much. Evidence from other populations (for which better data are available) suggests that correction factors of about 0.25 SD for the 5th percentile and 0.4 SD for the 95th percentile might be appropriate. The 50th percentile is probably very slightly overestimated.

5.2 Children (tables 4 to 8)

The stature data upon which tables 4 to 8 are based are taken from a survey conducted by the Department of Education and Science (DES 1972). The other dimensions are estimates.

The data are grouped for convenience into five age bands which span the years 3 to 18. Since children are growing continuously throughout this period, it necessarily follows that a 5th percentile eight-year-old (for example) will be smaller than the 5th percentile member of the 8 to 11 year age band; and a 95th percentile eleven-year-old will be larger than the 95th percentile member of the 8 to 11 year age band. For values broken down into one year age bands (based on the same data set) see Pheasant (1986) or DES (1985). Pheasant (1986) also has data for infants from birth to 3 years.

Note that the dimensions in tables 4 to 8 are those which are most likely to be useful for general design purposes. A British Standard which includes clothing design data for infants and children is currently in preparation.

5.3 Other populations

The simplest way of dealing with small anthropometric differences between populations is to use design limits, wider than the conventional 5th to 95th percentiles. Design limits based on the 2nd and 98th percentiles of the British dataset, would include the 5th to 95th percentiles for most other European and North American populations. Exceptions include the Swiss who are shorter and the Dutch who are taller. There may also be *samples* (i.e. subgroups) within these populations who are notably different. Detailed estimates for various European populations, the USA, Indians, Japanese and Hong Kong Chinese are given in Pheasant (1986).

Table 2. Anthropometric estimates for British adults (19 to 65 years)

Dimensions in mm. Percentiles rounded to nearest 5 mm, as appropriate.

		Men				Women			
		5th %le	50th %le	95th %le	SD	5th %le	50th %le	95th %le	SD
	Body weight (kg)	55	75	95	12	45	63	81	11
A	1 Stature	1625	1740	1855	70	1510	1610	1710	62
	2 Eye height	1515	1630	1745	69	1405	1505	1605	61
	3 Shoulder height	1315	1425	1535	66	1215	1310	1405	58
	4 Elbow height	1005	1090	1175	52	930	1005	1080	46
	5 Hip height	840	920	1000	52	740	810	880	43
	6 Knuckle height	690	755	820	41	660	720	780	36
	7 Fingertip height	590	655	720	38	560	625	690	38
B	8 Sitting height	850	910	970	36	790	850	910	35
	9 Sitting eye height	730	790	850	35	685	740	795	33
	10 Sitting shoulder height	540	595	650	32	505	555	605	31
	11 Sitting elbow height	195	245	295	21	185	235	285	29
	12 Thigh thickness	135	160	185	15	125	155	185	17
	13 Buttock-knee length	545	595	645	31	520	570	620	30
	14 Buttock-popliteal length	440	495	550	32	435	480	530	30
	15 Knee height	495	545	595	32	455	500	545	27
	16 Popliteal height	390	440	490	29	355	400	495	27
	17 Shoulder breadth (bideltoid)	420	465	510	28	355	395	435	24
	18 Biacromial breadth	365	400	435	20	325	355	385	18
	19 Elbow-elbow breadth	370	450	530	49	320	385	450	41
	20 Hip breadth	310	360	410	29	305	370	435	38
	21 Chest (bust) depth	215	250	285	22	205	250	295	27
	22 Abdominal depth	220	270	320	32	205	255	305	30
C	23 Shoulder-fingertip length	720	780	840	36	650	705	760	32
	24 Shoulder-elbow length	330	365	400	20	300	330	360	17
	25 Elbow-fingertip length	440	475	510	21	400	430	460	19
	26 Span	1655	1790	1925	83	1490	1605	1720	71
	27 Elbow span	870	945	1020	47	780	850	920	43
	28 Standing overhead reach	2040	2170	2300	79	1895	2010	2125	70
	29 Sitting overhead reach	1255	1355	1455	61	1150	1255	1340	58
	30 Forward reach	835	890	945	33	760	810	860	30
D	31 Hand length	173	189	205	10	159	174	189	9
	32 Hand breadth (metacarpal)	79	87	95	5	69	76	83	7
	33 Hand breadth (including thumb)	97	105	113	5	84	92	100	5
	34 Palm length	97	107	117	5	89	97	105	5

	35 Index finger length	64	72	80	5	60	67	74	4
	36 Index finger breadth	18	21	24	2	15	18	21	2
	37 Thumb breadth	20	23	26	2	16	19	22	2
	38 Hand thickness at palm	28	33	38	3	23	28	33	3
	39 Hand thickness (including thumb)	44	51	58	4	40	45	50	3
	40 Maximum grip diameter	45	52	59	4	43	48	53	3
E	41 Foot length	240	265	290	14	215	235	255	12
	42 Foot breadth	85	95	105	6	80	90	100	6
	43 Heel-ball length	170	190	210	11	160	175	190	10
	44 Ankle height	60	70	80	7	55	65	75	6
	45 Forefoot length	125	135	145	7	110	120	130	6
	46 Instep height	50	60	70	6	45	55	65	5
F	47 Head length	180	195	210	8	170	180	190	7
	48 Head breadth	145	155	165	6	135	145	155	6
	49 Head height	205	225	245	11	200	220	240	11
	50 Ear-crown	115	125	135	6	110	125	135	8
	51 Mouth-crown	165	180	195	9	150	170	190	11
	52 Ear-ear breadth	125	135	145	6	120	130	140	5
	53 Inter-pupillary breadth	56	63	70	4	52	59	66	4
	54 Maximum diameter from chin	240	255	270	8	255	235	245	7
	55 Nose-back of head	205	220	235	9	190	205	220	10
G	56 Maximum body breadth	480	530	580	30	355	420	485	27
	57 Maximum body depth	255	290	325	21	255	275	325	30
	58 Buttock-heel length	985	1070	1155	53	875	965	1055	55
	59 Popliteal height plus thigh thickness	540	600	660	35	500	555	610	33
	60 Popliteal height plus sitting elbow height	615	685	755	42	570	635	700	40
	61 Sitting elbow height minus thigh thickness	30	85	140	33	30	80	130	32
	62 Sitting eye height minus elbow height	495	545	595	31	455	505	555	29
	63 Elbow-fingertip length minus head length	245	280	315	21	220	250	280	19
	64 Forward reach minus abdominal depth	555	620	685	41	490	555	620	38
	65 Buttock-knee length plus forefoot length	675	730	785	34	635	690	745	33
H	66 Head girth	535	565	590	17	525	550	575	15
	67 Coronal arc	325	350	375	15	315	340	365	15
	68 Sagittal arc	350	380	410	18	325	350	375	15
	69 Neck girth	335	375	415	25	325	365	405	25

70 Chest (bust) girth	815	945	1075	80	795	955	1115	97
71 Underbust girth	—	—	—	—	655	790	925	83
72 Waist girth	660	810	960	90	540	705	870	99
73 Hip girth	865	965	1065	60	860	1005	1150	88
74 Thigh girth	465	550	635	51	470	565	660	57
75 Lower thigh girth	330	375	420	28	330	375	420	28
76 Knee girth	345	385	425	24	310	355	410	26
77 Knee girth (flexed)	395	435	475	24	375	420	465	28
78 Calf girth	315	355	395	25	300	345	390	26
79 Ankle girth	200	220	240	13	180	210	240	18
80 Lower ankle girth	240	265	290	15	220	255	290	21
81 Foot girth (ball)	215	245	275	17	200	225	250	16
82 Foot girth (heel-instep)	285	325	365	23	260	290	320	19
83 Scye girth	385	435	485	30	345	400	455	33
84 Biceps girth	250	305	360	32	215	285	355	42
85 Elbow girth (flexed)	315	345	375	19	270	295	320	16
86 Forearm girth	200	240	280	23	195	225	255	17
87 Wrist girth	165	175	190	10	140	155	170	10
88 Hand girth (palm)	200	215	230	10	170	185	200	9
89 Hand girth (across thumb)	230	250	270	12	200	215	230	10
90 Fist girth	270	295	320	14	230	250	270	11

I	91 Cervicale height	1385	1490	1595	64	1280	1370	1460	56
	92 Axilla height	1224	1320	1415	58	1340	1225	1210	52
	93 Sternale height	1315	1415	1515	62	1210	1305	1395	55
	94 Chest (bust) height	1175	1270	1365	58	1080	1170	1260	90
	95 Waist height	980	1065	1150	51	930	1010	1090	48

96 Crotch height	740	815	890	46	665	735	805	42
97 Gluteal height	720	795	770	46	650	720	790	41
98 Interscye	320	375	425	32	305	350	395	27
99 Chest breadth	275	310	345	21	235	265	295	18
100 Waist breadth	250	290	330	24	200	230	260	18
101 Bust breadth	—	—	—	—	160	205	250	28
102 Strap length	—	—	—	—	600	715	820	64
103 Shoulder length	145	170	195	15	100	120	140	12
104 Shoulder angle (degrees)	16	21	26	3	15	22	29	4
105 Sleeve length	810	875	940	40	735	790	835	30
106 Sleeve inseam	445	500	555	32	195	435	475	25
107 Waist front	360	410	460	30	305	355	405	30
108 Waist back	390	450	510	36	365	405	445	24
109 Crotch length	655	750	845	57	630	725	820	57
110 Vertical trunk circumference	1525	1645	1745	72	1435	1575	1715	84

Table 3. Anthropometric estimates for elderly people

Dimensions in mm. Percentiles rounded to the nearest 5 mm, as appropriate.

	Men				Women			
	5th %le	50th %le	95th %le	SD	5th %le	50th %le	95th %le	SD
1 Stature	1515	1640	1765	77	1400	1515	1630	70
2 Eye height	1410	1535	1660	76	1305	1420	1535	69
3 Shoulder height	1225	1345	1465	72	1130	1235	1340	65
4 Elbow height	935	1025	1120	57	860	945	1030	52
5 Hip height	785	875	965	55	700	780	860	49
6 Knuckle height	640	715	785	45	615	680	745	41
7 Finger height	550	620	690	42	520	590	660	43
8 Sitting height	760	835	910	45	695	775	855	50
9 Sitting eye height	655	725	795	43	600	675	750	47
10 Sitting shoulder height	480	545	610	39	435	505	575	44
11 Sitting elbow height	155	205	255	31	135	195	255	35
12 Thigh thickness	105	135	165	17	105	140	175	22
13 Buttock-knee length	510	565	620	34	490	545	600	34
14 Buttock-popliteal length	410	470	530	36	405	460	515	34
15 Knee height	455	515	575	35	430	580	630	30
16 Popliteal height	375	420	465	28	335	385	435	29
17 Shoulder breadth (fleshy)	380	420	460	25	335	375	415	23
18 Shoulder breadth (bony)	330	365	400	20	300	335	370	20
19 Elbow-elbow breadth	430	500	570	42	380	455	530	46
20 Hip breadth	345	410	475	40	320	395	470	45
21 Chest (bust) depth	215	255	295	23	205	285	305	30
22 Abdominal depth	275	340	405	40	250	325	400	45
23 Shoulder-fingertip length	670	735	800	39	605	665	725	36
24 Shoulder-elbow length	310	345	380	22	275	310	345	20
25 Elbow-fingertip length	410	450	490	23	370	405	440	22
26 Span	1540	1690	1840	91	1380	1515	1645	80
27 Elbow span	805	890	975	52	720	800	880	48
28 Standing overhead reach	1880	2025	2170	88	1740	1870	2000	80
29 Sitting vertical reach	1175	1285	1395	66	1085	1185	1285	60
30 Forward reach	780	845	910	38	700	760	820	35
31 Hand length	160	180	200	11	150	165	180	10
32 Hand breadth (metacarpal)	70	80	90	5	60	70	80	5
41 Foot length	225	250	275	15	200	225	250	14
42 Foot breadth	80	90	100	7	75	85	95	6
43 Heel-ball length	165	185	205	12	140	160	180	10
44 Ankle height	60	70	80	7	55	65	75	7
47 Head length	170	185	200	8	155	170	185	8
48 Head breadth	135	145	155	7	125	135	145	6

Table 4. Anthropometric estimates for 3 to 4-year-old British children

Dimensions in mm. Percentiles rounded to the nearest 5 mm, as appropriate.

	Boys				Girls			
	5th %le	50th %le	95th %le	SD	5th %le	50th %le	95th %le	SD
1 Stature	930	1020	1110	56	905	1010	1115	63
2 Eye height	825	915	1005	54	800	910	1020	68
3 Shoulder height	735	805	870	42	700	795	885	56
4 Elbow height	550	615	680	40	530	605	680	45
5 Hip height	415	480	546	39	415	485	550	41
6 Knuckle height	375	425	470	29	370	430	485	36
7 Fingertip height	305	350	395	28	295	355	410	34
8 Sitting height	535	585	630	28	520	575	625	32
9 Sitting eye height	430	475	520	28	405	465	520	35
10 Sitting shoulder height	315	355	395	24	300	350	395	28
11 Sitting elbow height	120	155	190	21	115	145	175	19
12 Thigh thickness	70	90	105	12	60	85	105	13
13 Buttock-knee length	275	315	350	23	275	320	360	25
14 Buttock-popliteal length	230	260	285	18	230	270	305	23
15 Knee height	265	300	335	22	255	300	340	25
16 Popliteal height	205	245	280	21	210	245	275	20
17 Shoulder breadth (bideltoid)	235	260	285	16	230	260	285	17
18 Biacromal breadth	205	230	255	14	205	235	260	15
20 Hip breadth	175	200	220	13	175	200	225	15
21 Chest depth	105	130	150	12	105	125	150	13
22 Abdominal depth	135	155	170	10	135	155	170	12
23 Shoulder-fingertip length	395	445	490	29	370	430	485	36
25 Elbow-fingertip length	240	270	295	17	235	265	295	20
26 Span	905	1010	1110	63	860	980	1095	70
27 Elbow span	475	530	590	35	450	515	585	41
28 Standing overhead reach	1030	1175	1315	85	1035	1165	1295	78
29 Sitting overhead reach	650	720	795	44	620	700	780	49
30 Forward reach	370	430	490	36	365	430	495	40
31 Hand length	100	115	125	8	100	115	130	9
32 Hand breadth (metacarpal)	50	55	60	4	45	55	60	5
41 Foot length	140	160	180	11	140	160	180	12
42 Foot breadth	60	65	70	4	55	65	70	5
47 Head length	170	180	190	7	155	165	175	7
48 Head breadth	130	140	150	6	120	130	140	6

Table 5. Anthropometric estimates for 5 to 7-year-old British children

Dimensions in mm. Percentiles rounded to the nearest 5 mm, as appropriate.

	Boys				Girls			
	5th %le	50th %le	95th %le	SD	5th %le	50th %le	95th %le	SD
1 Stature	1045	1170	1295	74	1040	1160	1280	74
2 Eye height	930	1055	1175	75	915	1045	1180	81
3 Shoulder height	820	925	1025	62	805	910	1020	64
4 Elbow height	620	705	790	51	610	695	780	52
5 Hip height	505	595	680	53	505	575	650	45
6 Knuckle height	420	480	545	38	420	495	565	43
7 Fingertip height	335	395	460	37	345	410	480	41
8 Sitting height	585	640	700	35	575	635	695	37
9 Sitting eye height	470	525	585	35	465	525	590	39
10 Sitting shoulder height	345	390	440	29	335	380	430	29
11 Sitting elbow height	135	170	205	23	130	160	195	21
12 Thigh thickness	75	95	120	14	75	95	120	14
13 Buttock-knee length	320	370	420	31	320	375	425	32
14 Buttock-popliteal length	255	305	350	29	270	315	360	28
15 Knee height	310	360	410	30	305	355	400	28
16 Popliteal height	250	295	340	27	250	220	330	24
17 Shoulder breadth (bideltoid)	250	285	325	23	245	285	320	23
18 Biacromial breadth	230	265	295	19	235	260	285	16
20 Hip breadth	185	215	250	20	185	220	260	22
21 Chest depth	110	140	170	18	110	140	170	18
22 Abdominal depth	135	160	185	16	135	165	195	19
23 Shoulder-fingertip length	445	505	570	29	425	490	555	40
25 Elbow-fingertip length	275	310	345	23	270	305	340	22
26 Span	1020	1160	1300	85	985	1125	1265	85
27 Elbow span	535	610	690	47	515	595	675	49
28 Standing overhead reach	1215	1390	1565	108	1210	1375	1540	101
29 Sitting overhead reach	715	810	905	57	700	790	885	56
30 Forward reach	430	495	560	38	420	485	545	37
31 Hand length	115	130	145	10	110	125	145	10
32 Hand breadth (metacarpal)	55	60	70	5	50	60	65	5
41 Foot length	160	185	210	14	155	180	205	14
42 Foot breadth	65	75	85	6	60	70	80	6
47 Head length	165	180	195	9	155	170	180	7
48 Head breadth	130	140	150	5	125	135	145	6

Table 6. Anthropometric estimates for 8 to 11-year-old British children

Dimensions in mm. Percentiles rounded to the nearest 5 mm, as appropriate.

	Boys				Girls			
	5th %le	50th %le	95th %le	SD	5th %le	50th %le	95th %le	SD
1 Stature	1220	1360	1495	85	1210	1360	1510	92
2 Eye height	1070	1215	1360	88	1095	1245	1395	92
3 Shoulder height	960	1090	1220	79	950	1090	1230	85
4 Elbow height	730	840	945	66	720	835	950	69
5 Hip height	620	715	810	57	605	705	805	60
6 Knuckle height	500	580	655	47	520	600	685	50
7 Fingertip height	410	485	555	44	425	505	585	48
8 Sitting height	645	710	775	39	645	715	780	42
9 Sitting eye height	535	595	650	36	540	605	675	41
10 Sitting shoulder height	395	450	500	32	380	440	500	37
11 Sitting elbow height	150	190	230	24	145	185	230	26
12 Thigh thickness	95	115	140	14	90	120	145	16
13 Buttock-knee length	390	450	510	36	390	455	525	41
14 Buttock-popliteal length	315	370	425	33	330	385	445	35
15 Knee height	375	430	485	34	370	430	485	35
16 Popliteal height	300	350	400	29	305	355	400	30
17 Shoulder breadth (bideltoid)	280	330	375	28	275	325	375	30
18 Biacromial breadth	265	300	335	20	260	300	335	23
20 Hip breadth	205	250	295	28	210	260	315	32
21 Chest depth	120	160	200	24	110	160	210	30
22 Abdominal depth	145	180	220	24	145	190	230	27
23 Shoulder-fingertip length	520	590	680	43	500	580	660	49
25 Elbow-fingertip length	320	365	405	27	310	360	410	31
26 Span	1205	1360	1520	96	1170	1335	1495	98
27 Elbow span	630	720	805	53	610	705	795	56
28 Standing overhead reach	1460	1645	1830	112	1440	1655	1865	129
29 Sitting overhead reach	830	940	1045	65	810	925	1040	70
30 Forward reach	495	565	635	42	490	570	645	48
31 Hand length	130	150	165	11	130	150	165	11
32 Hand breadth (metacarpal)	60	70	75	5	60	70	75	5
41 Foot length	185	215	240	16	185	210	235	15
42 Foot breadth	70	85	95	6	70	80	90	7
47 Head length	165	185	205	11	155	175	190	11
48 Head breadth	130	145	160	9	120	135	150	9

Table 7. Anthropometric estimates for 12 to 14-year-old British children

Dimensions in mm. Percentiles rounded to the nearest 5 mm, as appropriate.

	Boys				Girls			
	5th %le	50th %le	95th %le	SD	5th %le	50th %le	95th %le	SD
1 Stature	1385	1555	1725	104	1410	1545	1680	82
2 Eye height	1270	1440	1610	103	1295	1430	1565	82
3 Shoulder height	1120	1270	1425	92	1130	1255	1380	75
4 Elbow height	860	970	1085	68	865	965	1065	60
5 Hip height	740	835	935	59	715	800	880	49
6 Knuckle height	595	670	750	48	605	680	760	46
7 Fingertip height	485	560	635	46	495	570	650	46
8 Sitting height	705	795	885	55	725	805	880	47
9 Sitting eye height	595	685	770	53	620	695	765	45
10 Sitting shoulder height	445	510	580	40	450	510	565	36
11 Sitting elbow height	165	210	255	29	155	210	265	33
12 Thigh thickness	105	130	160	16	110	135	160	16
13 Buttock-knee length	460	525	590	39	470	530	585	35
14 Buttock-popliteal length	380	435	495	36	395	445	495	30
15 Knee height	440	500	560	37	435	485	530	30
16 Popliteal height	335	405	455	31	350	390	430	25
17 Shoulder breadth (bideltoid)	320	375	430	32	320	370	420	29
18 Biacromial breadth	295	340	380	26	300	335	370	22
20 Hip breadth	240	290	340	30	260	315	370	34
21 Chest depth	140	185	230	29	145	200	250	31
22 Abdominal depth	165	205	245	24	165	210	250	25
23 Shoulder-fingertip length	600	685	770	51	590	670	750	48
25 Elbow-fingertip length	365	420	475	33	370	410	450	25
26 Span	1380	1585	1790	125	1370	1535	1695	99
27 Elbow span	720	835	950	69	715	810	905	58
28 Standing overhead reach	1705	1910	2115	125	1695	1885	2075	116
29 Sitting overhead reach	945	1085	1225	86	940	1070	1205	80
30 Forward reach	570	650	735	50	570	640	710	43
31 Hand length	150	170	195	13	150	170	185	10
32 Hand breadth (metacarpal)	70	80	90	7	65	75	80	5
41 Foot length	215	245	275	17	210	230	255	13
42 Foot breadth	80	90	105	7	75	90	100	7
47 Head length	170	190	205	11	160	175	190	9
48 Head breadth	135	150	165	9	125	140	155	9

Table 8. Anthropometric estimates for 15 to 18-year-old British children

Dimensions in mm. Percentiles rounded to the nearest 5 mm, as appropriate.

	Boys				Girls			
	5th %le	50th %le	95th %le	SD	5th %le	50th %le	95th %le	SD
1 Stature	1610	1735	1855	75	1520	1620	1715	60
2 Eye height	1490	1615	1740	76	1410	1510	1610	60
3 Shoulder height	1310	1420	1530	67	1225	1315	1405	54
4 Elbow height	995	1080	1170	53	930	1005	1080	45
5 Hip height	835	915	995	49	750	820	885	40
6 Knuckle height	675	745	815	43	665	720	780	35
7 Fingertip height	555	625	695	43	550	610	665	35
8 Sitting height	825	900	970	44	800	855	905	33
9 Sitting eye height	715	785	850	41	690	740	790	31
10 Sitting shoulder height	520	580	635	35	500	550	595	28
11 Sitting elbow height	185	235	285	30	185	230	270	26
12 Thigh thickness	125	150	180	17	120	145	170	15
13 Buttock-knee length	530	580	630	30	510	555	600	28
14 Buttock-popliteal length	440	490	545	32	435	480	520	26
15 Knee height	500	545	590	28	455	500	540	26
16 Popliteal height	395	440	485	27	360	405	445	25
17 Shoulder breadth (bideltoid)	385	435	490	32	360	395	430	22
18 Biacromial breadth	345	385	420	23	330	355	385	17
20 Hip breadth	290	330	375	26	300	345	385	27
21 Chest depth	170	220	265	28	185	225	265	26
22 Abdominal depth	190	230	270	25	185	220	255	21
23 Shoulder-fingertip length	715	780	845	40	650	700	750	30
25 Elbow-fintertip length	435	470	510	23	395	425	455	17
26 Span	1630	1785	1935	92	1505	1610	1720	65
27 Elbow span	855	940	1025	52	785	850	915	40
28 Standing overhead reach	1955	2110	2260	93	1825	1965	2110	87
29 Sitting overhead reach	1120	1225	1330	64	1035	1135	1235	61
30 Forward reach	650	725	795	45	605	670	730	39
31 Hand length	170	190	205	9	160	175	190	9
32 Hand breadth (metacarpal)	80	90	95	5	70	75	80	4
41 Foot length	240	265	285	14	220	240	260	12
42 Foot breadth	90	100	110	6	80	90	100	5
47 Head length	185	200	210	8	170	180	190	8
48 Head breadth	145	155	165	6	135	145	155	5

6. Applications

Note. The data used in this section are all taken from table 2, with heel corrections as given in 3.5. Numbers in square brackets indicate the item number in the table.

6.1 Posture

Q. What is a good posture?

A. One which may be sustained with a minimum of muscular tension. Muscular tension results either from internal causes within the individual or from externally imposed mechanical loading (postural stress). The former is largely outside the control of the designer; the latter frequently results from poor anthropometrics. The principal sources of postural stress are as follows:

- The need to maintain the position of one or more unsupported parts of the body against the force of gravity. Holding the arms away from the body (either forward or to the sides) stresses the shoulder muscles; inclining either the head or trunk stresses the muscles of the spine.
- Twisted or asymmetric postures.
- The need to maintain joints near to the limits of their range of motion. 'Cramped' and 'stretched' postures stress muscles and ligaments and restrict blood flow. In general, postures which use the middle third of a joint's range are to be preferred.

Many ergonomists would strongly recommend equipment and furniture which gives the user freedom to adopt many different postures rather than fixing him in just one (e.g. the ability to alternate between sitting and standing when engaged in an activity over a period of time).

Individuals differ greatly in their responses to a particular postural stress. A stooped position or a poorly designed seat which is scarcely noticeable to one person may be cripplingly painful for another. We cannot assume that what is suitable for ourselves is necessarily suitable for other people.

6.2 Visual requirements

Visual information may be presented to the user of a product in the form of text or other symbols applied to labels, notices, dials, meters, computer screens, etc. Ergonomists refer to these collectively as 'visual displays'.

(a) Direction of gaze

The human visual field may be divided into central (foveal) and peripheral regions. Only the central portion, which is a few degrees of arc in extent, is suitable for complex visual tasks (reading text, recognizing shapes, etc.). We acquire information about our environment by a process of visual search or scanning, i.e. moving our eyes with respect to our heads or our heads with respect to our bodies. It is usual to describe the direction of gaze by means of the angle it subtends upwards or downwards from the horizontal (see figure 4).

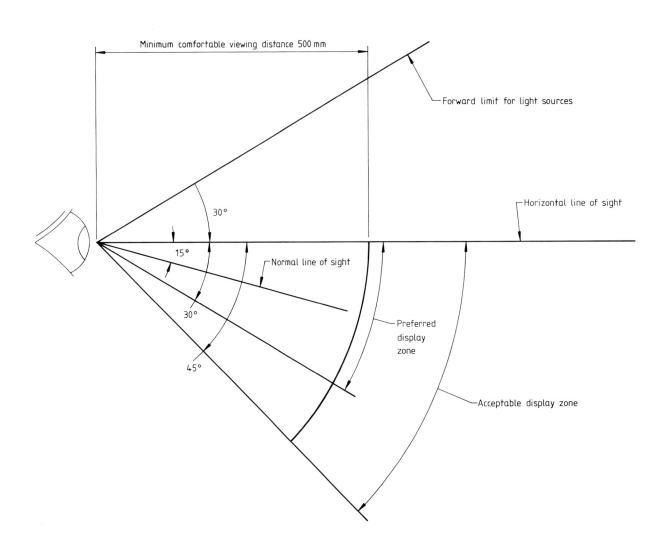

Minimum comfortable viewing distance 500 mm

Forward limit for light sources

Horizontal line of sight

30°

15°

Normal line of sight

30°

45°

Preferred display zone

Acceptable display zone

At rest, the eyes assume a downwards cast of about 15°, looking neither to the left nor to the right. This we call the *normal or resting line of sight*. The most important and frequently used visual displays should be within 15° of the normal line of sight. The preferred zone for visual displays is therefore between the horizontal and 30° downwards (within 15° on either side of straight ahead).

Less important displays may be located between 30° and 45° downwards. (Compromises should be made in favour of a display which is too low rather than one which is too high.)

A source of illumination which is located in front of a line of sight 30° upward from the horizontal is a potential source of glare.

(b) Visual distances

The eyes are relaxed when focused on infinity (or in practice, more than about 6 m distance). As an object approaches the eyes, an increasing muscular effort is required to view it. People characteristically read text at a distance of 400 mm (+ 50 mm). The minimum acceptable viewing distance for display instruments (such as dials and VDU screens) is 500 mm − and 700 mm is probably preferable. The maximum will be determined by the legibility of the display − which is determined by size, contrast, ambient lighting, etc. A simple rule of thumb is that conventional lettering in good illumination can be read at a distance of the height of the letters multiplied by 200.

Display instruments, as specified in BS 3693, are designed for reading at a distance of 1000 mm. Detailed recommendations for the design of various visual displays (text, instruments, public information symbols, etc.) are given in Pheasant (1987).

A British Standard dealing with VDUs and VDU workstations is currently in preparation.

6.3 Seats and seated workstations (see figure 5)

Nowhere are the applications of anthropometrics more crucial than in the design of seating. Since each application presents unique functional demands and design constraints, it is impossible to write a single specification for 'an ergonomically designed chair'. Rather, we shall concentrate on general principles. We shall employ the procedure known as the *method of limits* as described in 3.1. In each case we shall consider those anthropometric factors which might make a dimension 'too small', 'too large', or 'just right' and attempt to reach an appropriate compromise.

(a) Seat height (floor to sitting surface)

The optimum height for working chairs is often said to be 25 mm to 50 mm below popliteal height [16] − which suggests a range of 380 mm (5th percentile woman, shod, minus 25 mm) to 465 mm (95th percentile man, shod, minus 50 mm). An adjustable chair should include this range. In practice, people commonly set their chairs higher than this, because of the tables they use. In designing a working chair we must consider the task and the table on which it is performed. The desirable height for an easy chair may well be lower than this since people like to stretch out their legs.

In a non-adjustable seat, these considerations are academic. Seat heights should not exceed the popliteal height of the shortest user − and at more than 25 mm above popliteal height, seats rapidly become uncomfortable. A seat which is too high will be more tolerable if its front edge is suitably contoured. But excessively low seats result in slouched postures of the pelvis and lumbar spine, which are both inelegant and unhealthy. The lower a seat, the more difficult it is to stand up and sit down (a particular problem for elderly of infirm people). The shod popliteal height of a 5th percentile woman (400 mm) is a good compromise.

(b) Seat depth (front of sitting surface to backrest)

This shoud be treated as a reach dimension based on buttock-popliteal length [14]; 5th percentile female = 435 mm. Deeper seats will prevent shorter members of the population from fully utilizing the backrest; furthermore they increase the effort required to stand up and sit down. Tall people sometimes complain of seats, particularly easy chairs, being too short. It is not easy to see why − in many cases an inadequate backrest might be to blame (see below).

(c) Backrest

The function of the backrest is to give support to the weight of the trunk; but it must not impede the movements of the user's arms. When the latter is important, the backrest should stop at a level approximately 200 mm below the shoulders (95th percentile male = 450 mm; 5th percentile female = 305 mm). It is likely that this constraint has been overemphasized in the past − perhaps from a puritanical distrust of high-backed chairs in the working environment. The higher the backrest the better supported is the trunk. Many ergonomists would now recommend a backrest of 500 mm in height for office chairs (especially those used by VDU operators). The back of an easy chair should reach the level of the back of the head of a tall person. (Approximately equal to sitting eye height [9]; 95th percentile male = 850 mm.) If the backrest is too low, a tall person will slump down in the seat in an attempt to support his head; in so doing his buttocks will move forward along the seat giving the impression that it is not sufficiently deep.

Experimental studies have shown that stress to the spine will be reduced if the seat back has a convex pad in the lumbar region. In a non-adjustable seat the centre of this convexity should be 200 mm to 250 mm above the seat base. A lumbar pad which is too pronounced is probably worse than none at all. (A gentle 25 mm to 30 mm bulge in the lumbar region is about right.) Attempts to reflect the curve of the nape of the neck in the contours of a non-adjustable backrest are doomed to failure since this region is too variable in its location and too sharp in its curvature − a movable cushion is probably the best solution. (Can you work out what its range of adjustment should be?)

(d) Armrests

We cannot argue that an armrest which is too high is better or worse than one which is too low. An average value of male and female sitting elbow heights [11], 240 mm above the seat, seems reasonable.

(e) Seat breadth (single occupant)

Seats without arms do not require to support the entire breadth of the hips [20] but anything below about 400 mm is probably too small. A clearance of 460 mm between armrests will just be sufficient for a plump lady (99th percentile unclothed). Allowing some leeway, a minimum of 500 mm is desirable.

Width of knee-hole clearance beneath a desk should allow for a relaxed posture of the lower limbs; a minimum of 600 mm is required.

(f) Seat breadth (two or more occupants)

When two or more people must sit next to each other on bench style seats, shoulder breadth [17] is the appropriate clearance dimension. When two persons sit next to each other, the probability that they will both have greater than 95th percentile shoulders is only 1 in 400. (Can you work out why?) The space required for a 95th percentile pair of people is a little less than twice the 95th percentile shoulder breadth. (See A.5 in the appendix.)

Allowing 40 mm per person for outdoor clothing, two people require a clearance of 1075 mm at shoulder level and three require

1595 mm. Hence there is little to be gained from the omission of an intervening armrest. (These calculations do not allow for changes in posture or the social preferences of the persons concerned.)

(g) Seat angles

For postural support, a reclined sitting position is best − to relax your muscles you must be 'laid back'. Many working tasks prevent this desirable posture, and a 'perpendicular' position (similar to the standard sitting position described in 3.4) may be the best we can hope for. An office chair should provide for both these alternatives. In a comfortable laid-back position, the backrest makes an angle of 105° to 110° to the horizontal. For an easy chair this could be increased (with advantage) to 120° or more − although these steeper inclinations can make it difficult for the elderly or infirm to stand up and sit down.

In inclined sitting positions, there may be a tendency for the buttocks to slide forward. This may be counteracted by tilting the seat surface backwards by 5° to 10°.

(h) Table heights

The undersides of tables should provide clearance for the thighs and knees [12] and [15].The correct height for the table surface depends upon the task to be performed upon it. Ideally, keyboards should be at elbow height and writing surfaces about 50 mm above elbow height. Some people recommend a sloped writing surface (e.g. 15°) − with some means for preventing loose objects from rolling off.

Office desks are currently standardized at 720 (± 10) mm for writing and 670 (± 10) mm for typing (BS 5940).

This is a satisfactory compromise − but it is too low for some tall people, and some short people need a footstool. The only way around this difficulty would be to make an adjustable desk − and these are slowly coming in.

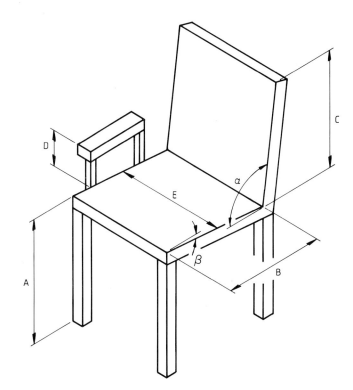

A – No more than popliteal height
B – No more than buttock-popliteal length
C – 500 mm for office chairs, approximately
   equal to sitting eye height for easy chairs
D – Average of male and female sitting
   elbow heights
E – Not less than 500 mm
α – 105° to 110° for office chairs, 120° for
   easy chairs
β – 5° to 10°

A typical dining table is about 780 mm high, and is used with a 470 mm seat. This gives a table surface 70 mm above the average sitting elbow height − which is very reasonable. But the seat is noticeably too high for the shorter person.

(i) Additional information

BS 5940: Part 1 deals with the dimensions of office furniture and workstations; BS 5873 deals with school furniture. These standards are summarized in Pheasant (1987). For a more detailed discussion of sitting posture and seat design, see Pheasant (1986).

6.4 Standing workspaces

(a) Reach

The volume of space which is 'within arm's length' is known as the *zone of convenient reach*. It may be defined by four anthropometric dimensions: standing overhead reach [28], forward reach [30], span [26] and fingertip height [7]. To draw the zone, take the 5th percentile values of the first three dimensions and the 95th percentile of fingertip height. The rest of the zone, as seen in elevation or plan, may be sketched in − as shown in figure 6. An alternative method employs the dimensions shoulder height [3], biacromial breadth [18] and shoulder-fingertip length [23]. The first two define the centre of the arc of rotation of the upper limb and the last defines its radius − see 7.4.

(b) Working height

The lower a working surface the more the user will have to stoop forward (typically bending from the waist). This imposes a severe postural load on the back muscles. If prolonged, this may cause back pain − and it will certainly exacerbate existing back problems − as any tall back pain patient who has to use a typical kitchen sink will tell you. Lifting or twisting actions, performed in a stooped position are particularly hazardous. On the other hand, as the working height increases, the muscle groups of the upper

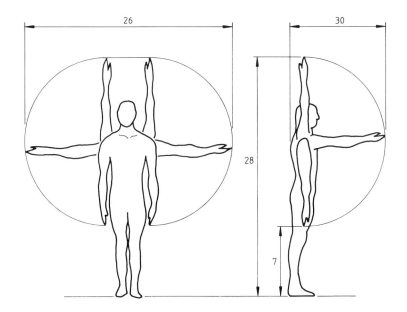

limbs have to work at an increasingly disadvantageous lever ratio − hence work may be more fatiguing.

The optimization of a working level proceeds by two stages. First, we must establish criteria which describe an appropriate level relative to anthropometric landmarks (stature, shoulder height, elbow height, etc.); secondly, we must apply the method of limits to these criteria in order to determine an actual working level.

The optimum height for performing a given task, depends upon the magnitude and direction of the forces involved, and the degree of precision (visual control) required. The following general guidelines may be helpful. See figure 7.

- For *manipulative tasks*, involving a moderate degree of force and precision, between 50 mm and 100 mm below elbow height.

- For *heavier tasks*, (especially involving downward pressure on the workpiece), a somewhat lower level is preferable — between 100 mm and 300 mm below the elbow, depending upon circumstances.
- For *delicate tasks*, 50 mm to 100 mm above the elbow (wrist supports may be desirable).
- For *lifting and handling tasks*, between knuckle height and elbow height. (The maximum lifting force can be exerted at knuckle height.)
- For *pushing and pulling actions*, about 100 mm below elbow height.
- For *storing and retrieving heavy objects*, from knuckle height to elbow height (or a little above) is the optimum. From elbow height to shoulder height is good for light objects and fair for heavy ones. Above eye level, storage is decreasingly useful. The highest acceptable level for unobstructed shelving is 150 mm less than vertical reach.
- For *wall-mounted controls*, between elbow height and shoulder height. (If these have associated displays, visual requirements must also be considered.)

To translate these criteria into actual design recommendations, the following steps are required:

(i) Decide upon the criteria which define an optimum working level. If this is not self-evident, a fitting trial may be required. Specify the criteria in terms of maximum and minimum distances above or below an anthropometric landmark (as above).

(ii) Discover the working height for which the greatest portion of the target population will be within the limiting criteria. (In fact this will be half way between the upper and lower limits for an average member of the target population — this is a consequence of the shape of the normal distribution.)

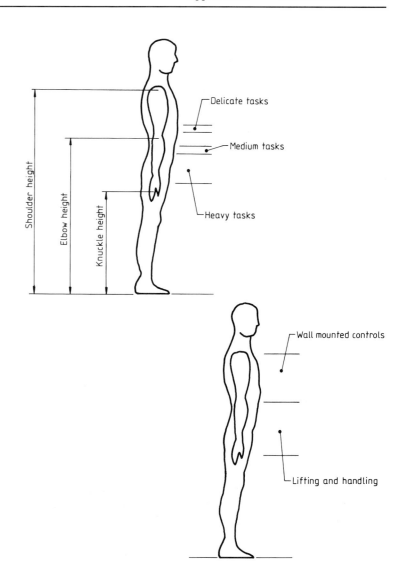

(iii) Calculate what proportion of the target population is accommodated within the criteria and what proportion is excluded (see section 2 and appendix for formula). Are these proportions acceptable? What will be the consequences for those who are excluded? Is it necessary to bias the level upward or downward?

(iv) Decide what workspace dimensions will achieve the desired working level (taking into account equipment to be used on top of work benches, etc.)

For a discussion of the application of ergonomics and anthropometrics to the design and standardization of domestic fixtures and fittings (in general) and kitchen equipment (in particular) see Pheasant (1987).

6.5 Safety distances

A safety guard or barrier will fulfill its purpose of separating people from hazards if either:

- apertures in the guard are sufficiently small to prevent the user from inserting his finger, hand, arm, etc. (as the case may be); *or*
- the distance between the guard and the hazard is sufficiently great for the latter to be safely out of reach (given the size of the aperture, etc.).

To fulfil these requirements the ordinary anthropometric criteria of clearance and reach must be reversed: hence aperture sizes must be based on the dimensions of the smallest probable user and reaches should be based on the largest. This allows us to calculate a *safety distance*: that is, a distance at which it is reasonable to conclude that the hazard is out of reach for most (if not all) members of a target population. (Given that the user

does not deliberately attempt to defeat the safety barrier by climbing over it, etc.)

BS 5304 deals with the safety of machinery. It includes an appendix of safety distances for an unspecified population of adult users. (The standard notes that the data should be used with caution if children might have access to the machinery concerned.) The safety distance for reaching upward is quoted as 2500 mm. Compare this with the data for standing overhead reach [28] given in table 2. (Take into account shoes, stretching, standing on tiptoe, etc.)

Figure 8 and table 9 show safety distances for reaching over barriers. Figures 9 and 10 show safety distances for reaching around edges and through apertures. These are all quoted from BS 5304. Again, compare these values with the data of table 2. The reach data in BS 5304 have recently been criticized by Thompson (1989).

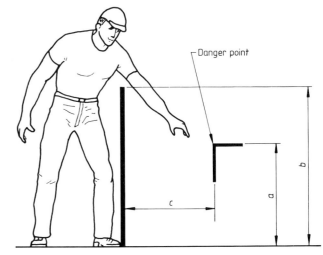

Table 9. Safety distances for reaching over barriers

Dimensions in mm

Distance of danger point from floor a	Height b of edge of barrier							
	2400	2200	2000	1800	1600	1400	1200	1000
mm	Horizontal distance c from hazard point							
2400	—	100	100	100	100	100	100	100
2200	—	250	350	400	500	500	600	600
2000	—	—	350	500	600	700	900	1100
1800	—	—	—	600	900	900	1000	1100
1600	—	—	—	500	900	900	1000	1300
1400	—	—	—	100	800	900	1000	1300
1200	—	—	—	—	500	900	1000	1400
1000	—	—	—	—	300	900	1000	1400
800	—	—	—	—	—	600	900	1300
600	—	—	—	—	—	—	500	1200
400	—	—	—	—	—	—	300	1200
200	—	—	—	—	—	—	200	1100

Fig 9. Safety distances for reaching round

Dimensions in mm.

		Safety distance r
Hand from root of finger to fingertip		mm $\geqslant 120$
Hand from wrist to fingertip		$\geqslant 230$
Arm from elbow to fingertip		$\geqslant 550$
Arm from arm-pit to fingertip		$\geqslant 850$

Fig 10. Reaching into and through square or circular apertures

Dimensions in mm. a aperture diameter or length of side, b safety distance from danger point

Fingertip

$4 < a \leqslant 8$
$b \geqslant 15$

Finger

$8 < a \leqslant 12 \quad 12 < a \leqslant 25$
$b \geqslant 80 \quad b \geqslant 120$

Hand to ball of thumb

$25 < a \leqslant 40$
$b \geqslant 200$

Arm to arm-pit

$40 < a < 150$ max
$b \geqslant 850$

6.6 Clothing design

The functional design of ready-to-wear clothing presents a complex set of anthropometric problems. In general, the designer's objectives will be to:

- provide an acceptable degree of fit with respect to a number of intercorrelated bodily dimensions;
- minimize the extent to which the garment hampers its wearer's movements;
- satisfy the maximum possible number of people with the minimum number of sizes in the range.

Size designation

With a few exceptions, current standards specify only the *designation* of clothing sizes — that is, the way they should be described in the shop. This allows the designer freedom to cut and style the clothes as fashion demands. The exceptions are certain garments, such as uniforms, which are not subject to rapid changes of fashion. A list of relevant standards will be found in the bibliography. The size designation system is based on a series of *control dimensions*: head girth [66], neck girth [69], chest girth [70], bust girth [70], underbust girth [71], waist girth [72], hip girth [73], stature [1], outside leg [95] and inside leg [96]. Certain specified combinations of these (given in centimetres) should appear on the garment's label — hence a man's shirt should be designated by neck girth and a woman's frock by bust girth, hip girth and stature. Examples are shown in figure 11.

Combinations of bust and hip girth define the familiar size code for women's garments, as given in table 10. Note that the dimensions used in this size designation system are all measurements of *the person the garment is intended to fit* — not measurements of the garment itself.

Table 10. Size codes and associated body measurements

Dimensions in mm, converted from dimensions in cm which appear on garment labels

Size codes	Body measurements			
	Hips		Bust	
	from	to	from	to
8	830	870	780	820
10	870	910	820	860
12	910	950	860	900
14	950	990	900	940
16	1000	1040	950	990
18	1050	1090	1000	1040
20	1100	1140	1050	1090
22	1150	1190	1100	1140
24	1200	1240	1150	1190
26	1250	1290	1200	1240
28	1300	1340	1250	1290
30	1350	1390	1300	1340
32	1400	1440	1350	1390

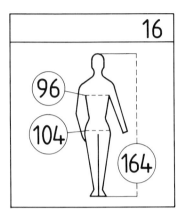
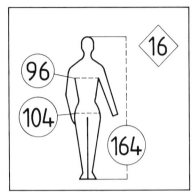

SIZE	16
BUST GIRTH	96
HIP GIRTH	104
HEIGHT	164

Despite its obvious good sense and manifest practical advantages, this system has by no means been universally adopted. (You should not find it hard to think of examples.)

Statistical aspects

The approach to a problem of clothing design might in principle be expected to proceed by the following stages:

(i) Select the control dimensions and other dimensions which are critical to the fit of the garment. Look up the relevant anthropometric data (in table 2 or elsewhere).

(ii) Determine the intercorrelations of these dimensions, (using table A.5 in the appendix).

(iii) Consider how close a fit you require with respect to each of these dimensions.

(iv) Determine the range of sizes required to satisfy an acceptably large proportion of the population with respect to the *most critical* dimension.

(v) Determine the combinations of dimensions which will satisfy the greatest number of people.

The first four stages are relatively simple; the last is more complicated. Highly correlated dimensions (such as bust girth and hip girth) present no real difficulties − by dividing a similar range of percentiles for each dimension into an equal number of intervals, the problem generally solves itself. (This, broadly speaking, is how the standard size coding system in table 10 operates.) Poorly correlated dimensions are much more problematic − neck size and sleeve length in shirts are a notorious example, as are the length and girth fittings of frocks and skirts. The statistical procedures required to deal with just two dimensions are not too difficult (see 7.7 for an example). But with three or more dimensions the calculations required increase in complexity, and rapidly become intractable.

Dynamic fit

Clothes must allow for movement. As you sit down the waist of your trousers rides up in the front and down at the back; as you bend your arm your sleeve rides up, and so on. Some typical allowances for movement are given in table 11.

Table 11. Dynamic fit − typical allowances for movement

Measurement	Action	Increment
Across elbow	Full flexion	85
Vertically across hip		
− front	90° flexion	−65
− back	90° flexion	85
− back	Full flexion	150
Vertically across knee		
− front	90° flexion	60
	Full flexion	105
Nape to coccyx	Full trunk flexion	100
Interscye	Reaching forwards with both arms	150

All increments in mm − from NASA (1978)

7. Worked examples

We shall conclude this outline of the principles of anthropometrics by working our way through some moderately complex examples. Our object will be to demonstrate the problem-solving strategies which an experienced user of anthropometrics might employ in specific design problems. In this way we will perhaps learn some of the 'tricks of the trade'.

In each case the solution has three essential phases:
(a)   identification of target population;
(b)   proposition of criteria;
(c)   application of the method of limits — this third phase being the most extensive.

7.1 Problem: To specify the desirable heights of a desk and chair to be used by copy typists (who use a conventional electric typewriter)

(i) What is our target population?
Most typists are female (although this may well change in the future). They tend to be young rather than old. We should therefore base our design on the female data of table 2, but adopt an upward bias when in doubt. Finally, we shall consider the consequences for male users and modify our thoughts if these are too appalling.

(ii) What are our criteria?
The seat should not be too high or too low (see 6.3(a)); the knees should clear the underside of the desk; the typewriter keyboard should be at elbow height or a little below it.

(iii) Where do we start?
This is a matter of intuition and/or experience. Shall the seat be fixed or adjustable? Probably adjustable — therefore start with the desk, since it is bound to be easier to specify variable levels with respect to fixed ones than vice versa. Adequate clearance must be provided beneath the desk.

There are two possible criteria for this: knee height [15] above the floor or thigh thickness [12] above the height of the seat. The latter is more generous; it may be derived from the combination dimension popliteal height plus thigh thickness [59]. This has a mean of 555 mm and a standard deviation of 33 mm. Using the method given in the appendix we calculate the 99th percentile and adding on 45 mm for shoes we arrive at a figure of 675 mm (rounded to the nearest 5 mm). This is probably too generous, since it is unlikely that a 99th percentile user will adjust her chair to exactly popliteal height. The optimum height for a seat is said to be 25 mm to 50 mm below popliteal height (see 6.3(a)). So the clearance required for the 99th percentile girl's thighs, is around $675 - 40 = 635$ mm.

This would be a suitable height for the underside of the desk. To improve our chances of accommodating the thickness of the desk plus the typewriter between the tops of the thighs and elbow level, the desk top should be as thin as possible, say 30 mm. It should be perfectly possible to span the width of the knee-hole with a structure this thin and retain adequate structural strength. The middle row of the keyboard of a typical conventional electric typewriter will lie some 70 mm above the desk top — but regrettably our brief is to design the furniture not redesign the typewriter.

(iv) This leaves us with an effective operating level of $635 + 30 + 70 = 735$ mm above the floor. Ideally the chair should be adjustable such that all users can bring their elbows to this level. Going downwards from 735 mm by 5th and 95th percentile female sitting elbow height [11] respectively suggests a seat which adjusts from 550 mm to 450 mm. What are the implications for thigh clearance? The underside of the desk minus 5th percentile female thigh thickness [12] is $635 - 125 = 510$ mm. There is little point in the chair adjusting to above this level.

Using the combination dimension, sitting elbow height minus thigh thickness [61] we may use the method given in A.2 in the appendix to calculate the proportion of the population who must type at *above* elbow height. The answer comes out at 74% − but we cannot improve this without redesigning the typewriter, which is not part of our brief.

(v) Are these seat heights satisfactory?
Our lowest seat height (450 mm) is above 5th percentile female shod popliteal height [16] = 390 mm − but it is likely that a girl with short legs will also have a small sitting elbow height and therefore wish to adjust her seat to a higher level rather than a lower one. The difference between the highest seat position and 5th percentile popliteal height is 145 mm − this discrepancy can be made up with a footrest. Nonetheless, provision should be made to lower the seat to a level which is closer to the 5th percentile popliteal height − 400 mm or 450 mm might be a sensible compromise. The height of the footrest should be variable. (There are three levels involved in this design − floor, seat and desk. To achieve a good anthropometric match, two out of the three must be variable.)

(vi) What are the consequences for male users?
The underside of the desk is greater than 95th percentile male shod knee height = 620 mm. The design should prove reasonably satisfactory for men.

(vii) To summarize, we recommend the following:
Desk underside = 635 mm;
Desk topside = 665 mm;

Seat adjustable from 400 mm or 425 mm to 515 mm;
Footrest(s) up to 145 mm.

Project work: Compare these dimensions with the current British Standard for office furniture (BS 5940:Part 1:1980). Go round some offices and measure the heights to which people have actually adjusted their chairs. Find out how comfortable they are and whether they have any aches or pains at the end of the working day.

7.2 Problem: To calculate the percentage of adult users who are accommodated (i.e. comfortably matched), by a dining room chair which is 450 mm in both height and depth (Assume the chair is satisfactory in all other respects.)

(i) The target population is adults as in table 2.

(ii) What are the criteria? The seat height should not be greater than popliteal height [16]. The seat depth should not be greater than buttock-popliteal length [14].

(iii) The calculation is a straightforward application of equation 4 from the appendix (as explained in section 2).

(iv) Deal with seat depth first. The distribution of buttock-popliteal length [14] in women has a mean of 480 mm and a standard deviation of 30. Therefore the given seat depth is $(480-450)/30 =$ one standard deviation below the mean. Therefore $z = 1$. Look this up in table A.2 in the appendix. The equivalent value of p is 16. Therefore the chair is too deep (i.e. more than buttock-popliteal length) for 16% of women.

Repeating the calculation for men, we find that $z = 1.41$; therefore $p = 8$.

(v) Now deal with the heights. Using popliteal height as the criterion (and not forgetting to add 45 mm for women's heels and 25 mm for men's) we get the following results: for women $z = 0.18$, $p = 57$; for men $z = -0.52$, $p = 30$; – and we conclude that these percentages of users would find the chair too high. Does anyone find it too low? The *optimum* height for a seat is said to be 25 mm to 50 mm below popliteal height. For the 95th percentile male, 50 mm below shod popliteal height is 440 mm. Our chair is higher than this so we don't have any problems in this direction.

(vi) Are these criteria too strict? We might choose to regard the figures we have calculated as the percentages of users who would find the chair 'slightly too high' or 'slightly too deep' respectively. Let us see what happens when we change the criteria by adding 25 mm (the anthropometric inch) in each case – so as to calculate the percentages for whom the chair is 'definitely too high' or 'definitely too deep'.

(vii) The results of the calculations are summarized as follows:

	Too low	Slightly too high	Definitely too high	Slightly too deep	Definitely too deep
Men (%)	0	30	8	8	1
Women (%)	0	57	23	16	3
Persons (%)	0	44	16	12	2

Will the people who find the seat too high also be the ones who find it too deep? Yes, to a large extent – since buttock-popliteal length and popliteal height are highly correlated.

Therefore we conclude that 44% of people will be slightly uncomfortable and 16% will be definitely uncomfortable.

Project work: Keep a diary, over the next week or so, of heights and depths of *all* the chairs you sit in. (Carry a tape measure with you at all times.) Note what the chairs are used for – and if a table is involved what its height is. What conclusions can you draw?

7.3 Problem: To determine the optimum height(s) of a kitchen worktop

(i) What is our target population?
Adult men and women of all ages; but mainly women. Therefore use data from table 2 with an emphasis on women.

(ii) What are our criteria?
The worktop should be at an appropriate distance below elbow height for the tasks which are to be performed. This raises a problem since many different tasks are performed on the kitchen worktop. Some of these are quite heavy and involve some downward force (e.g. kneading dough, rolling pastry), but the majority are relatively light. Considering the criteria for working heights given in 6.4(b), an optimum value of 100 mm below elbow height would seem an appropriate compromise. We might reasonably consider 25 mm on either side of this to be acceptable. Our design criterion then, is that the worktop should be between 75 mm and 125 mm below elbow height.

(iii) Look up elbow height [4] in table 2. Add on 25 mm for shoes (since people rarely wear high heels in the kitchen). The *best single compromise height* will be given by the 50th percentile female shod elbow height minus 100 mm. That is $105 + 25 - 100 = 930$ mm.

(iv) Is this single compromise value suitable for the population in general? Consider some limiting cases. For the 5th percentile woman the compromise height of 930 mm is 25 mm below shod elbow height (equals 955 mm). For the 95th percentile woman the compromise height is 175 mm below shod elbow height (equals 1105 mm). Both of these fall outside the design criteria (by 50 mm in each case). For a 95th percentile man the worktop would be 270 mm below shod elbow height (equals 1200 mm). We should expect the 5th and 95th percentile women to find our standard worktop a little too high and a little too low respectively. For the 95th percentile man it would be very much too low.

(v) The only way around this problem is to have worktops at a variety of heights. What should these be? The lowest we could reasonably require would be 75 mm below the 1st percentile female shod elbow height equals 850 mm. The highest would be 125 mm below 95th percentile male shod elbow height equals 1075 mm. A range of sizes, proceeding in 50 mm increments between these extremes, should satisfy just about everybody.

Project work: Consider whether the optimum height of the kitchen sink (measured to its rim) would be the same as the worktop height. Note that the effective working level at the sink is around 75 mm below its rim. Compare your conclusions with the recommendations of BS 3705 and BS 6222.

You might also care to think about the optimum height of a bathroom hand basin. How does this compare with the hand basins on the market?

A more detailed consideration of these matters will be found in Pheasant (1986).

7.4 Problem: To define the area on a table top that can be reached by a seated worker without undue effort

(i) What is the target population?
Adults of working age, presumably both men and women. Therefore use data from table 2.

(ii) What are the criteria?
The area is defined by the arc of rotation of the upper limb.

(iii) This is a reach problem, so we should base our calculations on 5th percentile female dimensions. We are not told anything about the heights of the table and seat, so let us assume that the table is at elbow height. (It cannot reasonably be lower − and if it is higher, the reach will be greater.)

(iv) Define the location of the shoulder joints in side elevation (see figure 12(a)). Since the table is at elbow height, the vertical distance of the shoulders above the table is given by shoulder-elbow length (SE) [24]. How do we determine the horizontal location of the shoulders? Since the worker is reaching forward, we may assume that her shoulders will be vertically above the table's edge.

(v) Calculate the radius R of the arc which is swept out on the table's surface by the upper limb. This is calculated from shoulder-elbow length (SE) [24] and shoulder-fingertip length (SF) [23] by Pythagoras' theorem.

$$SF^2 = SE^2 + R^2$$

For simplicity use 5th percentile values throughout.

(This is not quite the same as a true 5th percentile reach but the difference is minimal. Can you work out why?)

Hence $R = \sqrt{(650^2 - 300^2)} = 577$ mm

(vi) Draw the arcs of rotation in plan view, as shown in figure 12(b). The centres of rotation are the points S_1 and S_2 which are vertically below the shoulder joints. The distance between them is given by 5th percentile shoulder breadth (biacromial) [18] = 325 mm. The two arcs intersect at point M, in the mid-line plane of the body, and they cut the line of the table's edge at A_1 and A_2.

The total area of convenient reach is defined by the arcs $A_1 M$ and $A_2 M$.

(vii) Within the overall area of convenient reach there is a smaller optimum working area. This is defined by the arc of rotation of the forearm, the radius of which is elbow-fingertip length (EF) [25]; 5th percentile woman = 400 mm. The forearm arcs intersect in the mid-line plane at N. Draw perpendiculars to the table's edge at S_1 and S_2. The optimum area is defined by arcs drawn from N to points B_1 and B_2, such that lines $B_1 S_1$ and $B_2 S_2$ subtend angles of 25° with the perpendiculars. (A more exact analysis may be found in Pheasant 1986.)

Project work: Draw a composite diagram to show the zone of convenient reach at different heights above and below the elbow. (If you are familiar with computers, you should not find it hard to write a program to do this.) How might such data be applied in the design of a motor car (for example)?

7.5 Problem: To design a desk top computer, incorporating keyboard and screen

The screen is 250 mm by 185 mm; the keyboard is 260 mm by 100 mm.

(i) What is our target population?
Males and females of all ages, therefore use table 2.

(ii) What are our criteria?
The keyboard shall be at elbow height; the screen shall be located according to the provisions of 6.2.

(iii) We shall tackle this problem graphically; the side elevation will be the most informative view (see figure 13).

Let point A represent the centre of the keyboard.

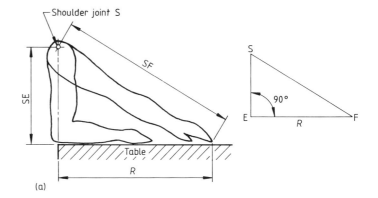

(a)

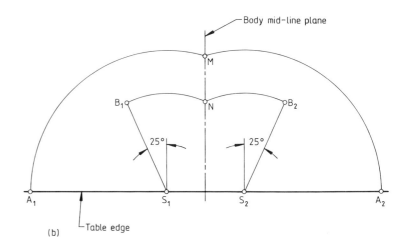

(b)

Draw a horizontal line through A and mark off distances AB and AC equal to 5th percentile female and 95th percentile male values for the combination dimension elbow-fingertip minus head length [63]. Draw verticals through these points such that BD and CE equal the 5th percentile female and 95th percentile male values of the combination dimension sitting eye height minus elbow height [62]. Hence points D and E represent two extreme locations for the user's eyes. (Note that the line ED approximately describes the eye positions of people of average bodily proportions. In fact, since people vary in shape as well as size, eye positions will be scattered about this line. Think of the eye positions forming an elliptical cloud; the long axis of the ellipse is ED.)

(iv) Draw horizontals EF and DG; then draw lines EH and DJ such that angle FEH = angle GDJ = 30°. These represent optimum viewing zones for eye positions E and D. The area bounded by the angle GKH is common to both − it is here that the screen should be located (see 6.2(a)).

(v) Draw arcs of radius 500 mm with centres E and D. The screen should not intrude within these arcs (see 6.2(b)).

(vi) Having defined limits which are acceptable for a large proportion of the population, we can complete our design by optimally matching the layout to an 'average user'. Point L represents the 50th percentile unisex eye position. Draw the line LM 15° down from the horizontal. Set the screen at right angles to this line 600 mm to 700 mm from L. Now check that the visual distances from E and D are still acceptable.

Project work: Consider the following questions. Should the keyboard and screen really be housed in the same unit, or would it be better for them to be separate? Do people really wish to operate computers in the standard sitting position? If not, how should VDU workstations be modified?

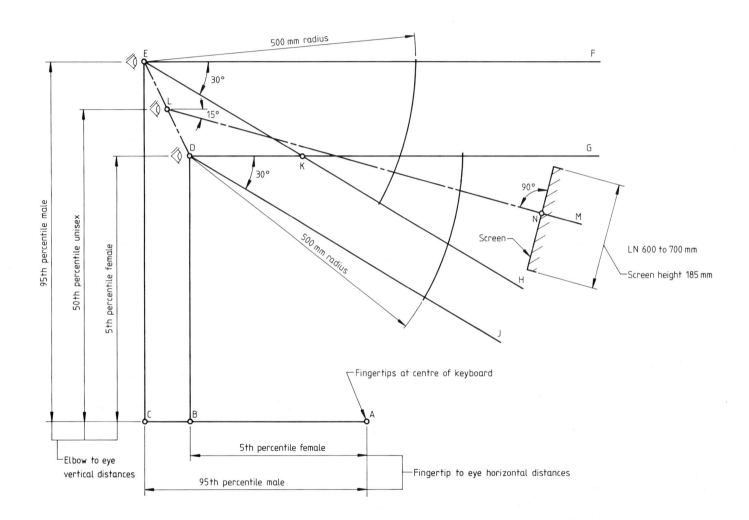

500 mm radius

30°

15°

30°

500 mm radius

90°

Screen

LN 600 to 700 mm

Screen height 185 mm

95th percentile male

50th percentile unisex

5th percentile female

Elbow to eye vertical distances

Fingertips at centre of keyboard

5th percentile female

95th percentile male

Fingertip to eye horizontal distances

7.6 Problem: To specify the height of a lectern for use in a college lecture theatre

(i) What is the target population?
Men and women of all ages; therefore use table 2.

(ii) What are our criteria?
The lecturer must be able to see the audience and vice versa. The height of the lectern must be convenient for both reading and page turning – but these relationships are not easy to specify numerically. We shall therefore proceed experimentally; we shall conduct a *fitting trial*.

(iii) Procedure.
Ten design students (five boys, five girls) acted as subjects. The only equipment used in the mock-up was an adjustable music stand and a wooden box on which to place it for higher settings. A manuscript, hand written on A4 paper, was placed on the music stand.

Each subject took his or her own time to find three height settings: the highest he or she would personally find acceptable; the lowest acceptable; and the level personally considered to be the optimum. (Ideally two sets of decisions should be made – one ascending and the other descending. The results should then be averaged.) Height measurements were taken to the centre of the A4 sheet. The subject's stature was measured – barefoot for comparison with other surveys. The fitting trial was performed shod.

(iv) Data analysis – simple version.
The subjects are arranged in table 12 in ascending order of stature. The mean, minimum and maximum values at the bottom of the table have been rounded to the nearest 5 mm.

The minimum recorded value of the maximum acceptable height was 1235 mm. The maximum recorded value of the minimum acceptable height was 1110 mm. The average value of the optimum height fell neatly between these limits at 1165 mm.

The lectern should therefore be designed such that the centre of a page of manuscript is 1165 mm above the floor.

(v) Data analysis – complex version.
The above reasoning would be impeccable if the subjects in the experiment were representative of the target population. But the stature data tell us that our subjects are taller than the population in general. (This is not particularly surprising.) There are a number of ways of dealing with this. The simplest is to scale down the measured optimum by multiplying it by the ratio of the average stature of the target population to the average stature of the experimental subjects. Hence, scaled optimum = $1165 \times 1675/1715 = 1138$ mm. (Note that 1675 mm is the unisex average stature of the target population.) We need to check that this is still within the tolerance limits for the extremes – so these need to be scaled down too. Multiply the upper limit by the ratio of the target 5th percentile female stature to the minimum recorded stature: $1235 \times 1510/1625 = 1148$ mm. Multiply the lower limit by the ratio of the target 95th percentile to the maximum recorded stature: $1110 \times 1855/1864 = 1104$ mm. Our scaled optimum falls within these limits so we round it to the nearest 5 mm and take 1140 mm as our final choice.

Table 12. An example of a fitting trial

Subject	Stature	Maximum acceptable height	Minimum acceptable height	Optimum height
Lucy	1625	1305	895	1175
Jane	1630	1235	940	1175
Claire	1635	1255	925	1160
Annetta	1670	1348	1112	1192
Amanda	1670	1250	1040	1185
Tony	1670	1300	975	1170
John	1760	1400	955	1195
Doug	1770	1315	910	1085
James	1835	1450	975	1165
Stuart	1865	1460	1060	1160
Mean	1715	1330	980	1165
Standard deviation	88	81	71	31
Minimum	1625	1235	895	1085
Maximum	1865	1460	1110	1195

7.7 Problem: To select a suitable range of collar sizes and sleeve lengths for men's shirts

The statistical concepts involved in this problem are a little more complicated than we have used so far. This example is really only for the mathematically intrepid reader. Before proceeding, it might help to read through A.3 in the appendix on the correlation coefficient.

We shall work in inches, since when it comes to men's shirts these are much more familiar than standard metric units. (Note that 1 inch = 25.4 mm.) The results of the calculation are shown in figure 14, which is labelled in both inches and millimetres.

(i) For a comfortable fit, the collar size (measured from button to buttonhole) should be from $\frac{1}{2}$ inch to 1 inch greater than the anatomical circumference of the neck [69]. The bottom two scales show the normal range of collar sizes (14 to $17\frac{1}{2}$) and the neck girths they will fit (13 to 17). For $\frac{1}{2}$ inch intervals of neck girth calculate the equivalent percentile − using equation 1 from the appendix and the data from table 2 (converted to inches). The range chosen will fit the 96% of the male population who are between the 3rd and 99th percentile in neck girth. The percentage of men requiring any given collar size is given by the difference between the percentile equivalents of its limiting neck girths. Hence a $15\frac{1}{2}$ collar is suitable for $58 − 38 = 20\%$ of the population, etc.

(ii) Compute the regression of sleeve length [105] on neck girth [69]. First we find the correlation coefficient from table A.5. Anthropometric sleeve length, measured from the backbone to the wrist, is a combination of a trunk breadth and a limb length. The correlation for girths against breadths equals 0.56 and for girths against lengths equals 0.27. Choose a half-way value of $r = 0.43$. Substituting the relevant values into equations 9 and 10 gives a regression equation of sleeve length $= 0.676$ neck girth $+ 24.4$; with a standard error of 1.39 inches. (Don't give up if this paragraph is too difficult − the rest is easier to follow.)

(iii) The oblique line drawn across figure 14 represents the above regression equation. That is, it denotes the average value of anthropometric sleeve length for men of a particular neck girth. Assume that a shirt may be deemed to fit if its actual sleeve length (from mid-back to cuffs) is within ± 1 inch of the anthropometric sleeve length of the man wearing it. The regression line shows the shirt sleeve length for any neck girth (or collar size) which will satisfy the largest number of users. We will call this the 'standard' fitting. Using the standard error (1.39) we calculate that 1 inch on either side of the mean is equivalent to $z = \pm \ 1/1.39 = \pm \ 0.72$. Looking this up in table A.2 we find that the standard sleeve length, for any given neck girth, will satisfactorily fit the 52% of men who are between the 24th and 76th percentiles.

(iv) We may also calculate that the provision of a 'long' and 'short' sleeve length 2 inches either side of the standard fitting, will each satisfy a further 22% of men. The three sleeve length fittings, for each collar size, are drawn as boxes in the diagram. The figure in each box indicates the number of men, per thousand in the population, for whom the particular combination of collar size and sleeve length will be a satisfactory fit.

Figure 14

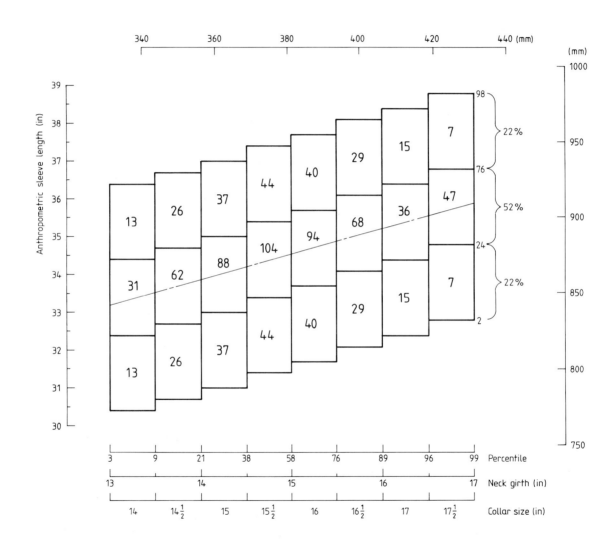

Appendix. Statistical tables and formulae

A.1 The standard deviation

The statistical parameter of the normal distribution known as 'the standard deviation' (s) is defined mathematically as follows:

$$s = \sqrt{\left[\frac{\Sigma\,(x-m)^2}{n-1}\right]} \tag{1}$$

where m is the mean, x is any individual value of the dimension with which we are concerned, and n is the number of subjects in the sample.

You may care to think of s as the root mean squared (rms) deviation. These days, you can cheaply purchase a pocket calculator, which directly calculates the mean and standard deviation of a set of numbers. But should you ever need to do this longhand, or write a program for it, it is worth remembering that:

$$\Sigma\,(x-m)^2 = [\Sigma x^2 - (\Sigma x)^2]/n \tag{2}$$

As a first approximation, the standard deviation of a sample of n subjects may be estimated from its maximum and minimum observed values, by the equation:

$$s = (\text{max}-\text{min})/2d \tag{3}$$

where d is a parameter known as the mean deviation of the largest member of the sample – it is given in table A.1 as a function of n.

A.2 Tables of the normal distribution

Knowing the mean and standard deviation of any normal distribution we may calculate the value x_p of any percentile we choose by the equation:

$$x_p = m + zs \tag{4}$$

where p is the percentile concerned and z is a constant which we look up in table A.2. (z is known as the 'standardized normal deviate'.)

Examples:
To calculate the 99th percentile of male stature

From table 2, mean = 1740 mm; s = 70 mm

For p = 99, z = 2.33 (from table A.2)

99th percentile stature = 1740 + (2.33 × 70) = 1903 mm

To calculate what percentage of men are taller than 1800 mm

z = (1800 − 1740)/70 = 0.86

p = 81; therefore 19% of men are taller than 1800 mm.

The ordinate (q) of the normal curve (that is, the height of the curve above the horizontal axis) is given in table A.3, as a function of z. The ordinate for the mean (z = 0) has been arbitrarily set at 1000. These figures represent the relative probability (or relative frequency) of encountering a person of a particular size. In table A.4, q is given for selected values of p.

A.3 The correlation coefficient (r)

The correlation coefficient is an index of how closely two variables (such as body dimensions) are related to each other.

Consider two normally distributed variables x and y, having means and standard deviations m_x, m_y, s_x and s_y respectively. Their correlation coefficient (r) is given by:

$$r = \frac{\Sigma(x-m_x)(y-m_y)}{\sqrt{[\Sigma(x-m_x)^2\,\Sigma(y-m_y)^2]}} \qquad (5)$$

or

$$r = s_{xy}/(s_x s_y) \qquad (6)$$

$$s_{xy} = [\Sigma(x-m_x)(y-m_y)]/n \qquad (7)$$

As observed in section 2, body dimensions fall into categories of lengths, breadths, girths, etc. Typical values for the correlations between categories are given in table A.5.

The figures tabulated are median or 50th percentile values of the correlations between the various pairs of dimension in each category, as given in NASA (1978) and Roebuck *et al* (1975).

A.4 Regression

For any given value of x, the values of a correlated dimension (y) will be normally distributed.

The mean of this distribution is given by the equation:

$$y = ax + b \qquad (8)$$

where

$$a = r\,(s_y/s_x) \qquad (9)$$

and

$$b = m_y - am_x \qquad (10)$$

Furthermore, the standard deviation of y for any given value of x, is given by:

$$SE_y = s_y\sqrt{(1-r^2)} \qquad (11)$$

which is known as the standard error of the estimate.

We may think of SE_y as being the portion of S_y which remains, after the variation in x has been accounted for; or alternatively, as the standard deviation of y in a sample of people *who all have the same value of* x. SE_y can therefore be used to calculate percentiles in the usual way. Table A.6 shows values of $\sqrt{(1-r^2)}$ (i.e. SE_y/S_y) for the values of r given in table A.5.

Example:
Estimate the likely limits of the knee height of a man who is 1800 mm in stature

From table 2, $m_x = 1740$ mm; $s_x = 70$mm
$m_y = 545$ mm; $s_y = 32$ mm

(where x is stature and y is knee height).

From table A.5, $r = 0.84$ (since knee height is in group C)
$a = 0.84 \times 32/70 = 0.38$
$b = 545 - (0.38 \times 1740) = -116$

If $x = 1800$ mm, $y = (0.38 \times 1800) - 116 = 568$ mm.

Furthermore, from table A.6 the standard deviation of this estimate is
$SE_y = 0.543 \times 32 = 17$ mm.

Hence there is a 90% chance that a man whose stature is 1800 mm, will have a knee height in the range of $568 \pm (1.645 \times 17) = 540$ mm to 596 mm (since ±1.645 are the z scores for the 5th and 95th percentiles).

A.5 Combination dimensions

To calculate the mean and standard deviation of a combination dimension, which is the sum of two others, or the difference between two others, use the following equations:

$$m_{(x+y)} = m_x + m_y \qquad (12)$$

$$s_{(x+y)} = \surd(s_x^2 + s_y^2 + 2rs_x s_y) \tag{13}$$

$$m_{(x-y)} = m_x - m_y \tag{14}$$

$$s_{(x-y)} = \surd(s_x^2 + s_y^2 - 2rs_x s_y) \tag{15}$$

These equations were used to calculate the combination dimensions 59 to 65 in table 2. Exact values of r (from Roebuck *et al* 1975) were used, rather than the typical values in table A.5.

Example:

To calculate the 5th and 95th percentile male values of the distance between the shoulder and the wrist.

This is the difference between shoulder-fingertip length [23] and hand length [31]. From table 2, $m_x = 780$ mm; $s_x = 36$ mm; $m_y = 189$ mm; $s_y = 10$ mm (where x is shoulder-fingertip length and y is hand length). From table A.5, $r = 0.34$ (row G, column C).

$$m_{(x - y)} = 780 - 189 = 591 \text{ mm}$$

$$s_{(x - y)} = \surd[36^2 + 10^2 - (2 \times 0.34 \times 36 \times 10)] = 34 \text{ mm}$$

For the 95th and 5th percentiles, $x = \pm 1.65$ (from table A.2). The 95th and 5th percentile values of shoulder-wrist length are given by $591 \pm (1.645 \times 34) = 647$ mm and 535 mm.

In the special case when $r = 0$, $m_x = m_y$ and $s_x = s_y$. Then $m_{(x+y)} = 2\,m_x$ and $s_{(x+y)} = s_x \surd 2$. This is useful in calculating the space required by combinations of people.

More generally, for n people sitting in a row, the mean and standard deviation (m' and s') of their combined breadth or depth, etc. is given by:

$$m^1 = nm \tag{16}$$

$$s^1 = s\surd n \tag{17}$$

(See 6.3 (f) for an application of these equations to the design of seats for more than one occupant.)

Table A.1. Mean deviation of the largest member of a sample

n	d	n	d
2	0.56	14	1.70
3	0.85	16	1.76
4	1.03	18	1.82
5	1.16	20	1.87
6	1.27	25	1.97
7	1.35	30	2.04
8	1.42	35	2.11
9	1.49	40	2.16
10	1.54	45	2.21
12	1.63	50	2.25

Table A.2. Percentiles p and corresponding z values for the normal distribution

p	z	p	z	p	z	p	z	p	z
1	-2.33	21	-0.81	41	-0.23	61	0.28	81	0.88
2	-2.05	22	-0.77	42	-0.20	62	0.31	82	0.92
3	-1.88	23	-0.74	43	-0.18	63	0.33	83	0.95
4	-1.75	24	-0.71	44	-0.15	64	0.36	84	0.99
5	-1.64	25	-0.67	45	-0.13	65	0.39	85	1.04
6	-1.55	26	-0.64	46	-0.10	66	0.41	86	1.08
7	-1.48	27	-0.61	47	-0.08	67	0.44	87	1.13
8	-1.41	28	-0.58	48	-0.05	68	0.47	88	1.18
9	-1.34	29	-0.55	49	-0.03	69	0.50	89	1.23
10	-1.28	30	-0.52	50	0	70	0.52	90	1.28
11	-1.23	31	-0.50	51	0.03	71	0.55	91	1.34
12	-1.18	32	-0.47	52	0.05	72	0.58	92	1.41
13	-1.13	33	-0.44	53	0.08	73	0.61	93	1.48
14	-1.08	34	-0.41	54	0.10	74	0.64	94	1.55
15	-1.04	35	-0.39	55	0.13	75	0.67	95	1.64
16	-0.99	36	-0.36	56	0.15	76	0.71	96	1.75
17	-0.95	37	-0.33	57	0.18	77	0.74	97	1.88
18	-0.92	38	-0.31	58	0.20	78	0.77	98	2.05
19	-0.88	39	-0.28	59	0.23	79	0.81	99	2.33
20	-0.84	40	-0.25	60	0.25	80	0.84	99.5	2.58

Table A.3. The ordinate (q) of the normal distribution as a function of the standardized normal deviate (z)

z	0	0.1	0.2	0.3	0.4	0.5	0.6	0.7	0.8	0.9
0	1000	995	980	956	923	882	835	783	726	667
1	606	543	486	430	375	325	278	236	198	164
2	135	110	89	71	56	44	34	26	20	15
3	11	8	6	4	3	2	2	1	1	1

Table A.4. The ordinate (q) of the normal distribution, for selected values of p

p	0.1	0.5	1	2.5	5	10	15
q	8	36	67	146	258	440	585
p	99.9	99.5	99	97.5	95	90	85
p	20	25	30	35	40	45	50
q	701	796	872	929	969	992	1000
p	80	75	70	65	60	55	50

Table A.5. Typical values of the correlation coefficient *(r)* **for groups of anthropometric measures**

Group		A	B	C	D	E	F	G	H
A	Stature	–							
B	Weight	0.51	–						
C	Heights, reaches and limb lengths	0.84	0.46	0.63					
D	Trunk breadths and depths	0.27	0.77	0.24	0.59				
E	Trunk girths (including neck)	0.29	0.79	0.27	0.56	0.54			
F	Limb breadths and girths	0.25	0.78	0.29	0.50	0.48	0.54		
G	Hand and foot	0.42	0.41	0.34	0.23	0.26	0.31	0.47	
H	Head and face	0.23	0.26	0.17	0.17	0.16	0.17	0.19	0.16

Table A.6. Typical values of $\sqrt{(1-r^2)}$ **(%) for groups of anthropometric measures. Note that** $\sqrt{(1-r^2)} = SE_y/S_y$

Group		A	B	C	D	E	F	G	H
A	Stature	–							
B	Weight	86.0	–						
C	Heights, reaches and limb lengths	54.3	88.8	77.7					
D	Trunk breadths and depths	96.3	63.8	97.1	80.1				
E	Trunk girths (including neck)	95.7	61.3	96.3	82.8	84.2			
F	Limb breadths and girths	96.8	62.6	95.7	86.6	87.7	84.2		
G	Hand and foot	90.8	91.2	94.0	97.3	96.6	95.1	88.3	
H	Head and face	97.3	96.6	98.5	98.5	98.7	98.5	98.2	98.7

Bibliography

Also by the author

Pheasant S T. 1987. *Ergonomics − standards and guidelines for designers* PP 7317. London: British Standards Institution
An extensive compilation of British and International Standards together with other guidelines dealing with all aspects of ergonomics.

Pheasant S T. 1986. *Bodyspace − Anthropometry, Ergonomics and Design.* London: Taylor and Francis
A detailed treatment of the anthropometric side of ergonomics, suitable both for beginners and for the more advanced student. Includes a large collection of anthropometric data and a more extended treatment of seating, posture, workstation design and other topics covered in this volume.

Other useful books about ergonomics and anthropometrics

Grandjean E. 1988. *Fitting the task to the Man − A text book of Occupational Ergonomics,* 4th edition. London: Taylor and Francis

Grandjean E. 1973. *Ergonomics in the Home.* London: Taylor and Francis

McCormick E J and Saunders M S. 1982. *Human Factors in Engineering and Design.* New York: McGraw-Hill

Oborne D J. 1987. *Ergonomics at Work,* 2nd edition. Chichester: John Wiley

Roebuck J A; Kroemer K H E and Thomson W G. 1975. *Engineering Anthropometry Methods.* Chichester: John Wiley

Singleton W T (ed). 1982. *The Body at Work − Biological Ergonomics.* Cambridge University Press

Sources of anthropometric data

Damon A; Stoudt H W and McFarland R A. 1966. *The Human Body in Equipment Design.* Cambridge, Mass: Harvard University Press

DES. 1972. *British School Population Dimensional Survey.* Building Bulletin 46. Department of Education and Science. London: HMSO

DES. 1985. *Body Dimension of the School Population.* Building Bulletin 62. Department of Education and Science. London: HMSO

Gooderson C Y and Beebee M. 1976. *Anthropometry of 500 infantrymen 1973-1974.* Report APRE 17/76. Army Personnel Research Establishment, Farnborough, Hants

Haslegrave C M and Hardy R N. 1979. *Anthropometric Profile of the British Car Driver.* Motor Industry Research Association, Nuneaton, Warwickshire

Kember P; Ainsworth L and Brightman P. 1981. *A Hand Anthropometric Survey of British Workers.* Cranfield Institute of Technology, Bedfordshire

Kemsley W F F. 1957. *Women's Measurements and Sizes.* Cheltenham Press

ICE. 1983. *Seating for Elderly and Disabled People, Report No 2 − Anthropometric Survey.* Institute for Consumer Ergonomics, University of Technology, Loughborough

Knight I. 1984. *The Heights and Weights of Adults in Great Britain.* London: HMSO

NASA. 1978. *Anthropometric Source Book.* NASA publication No 1024 US National Aeronautics and Space Administration, Washington DC

Thompson D. 1989. Reach distance and safety standards. *Ergonomics*, **32**, 1061-1067

WIRA. 1980. *British Male Body Measurements.* WIRA Clothing Services, Leeds

British Standards cited in the text

BS 3666   Specification for size designation of women's wear

BS 3693   Recommendations for the design of scales and indexes on analogue indicating instruments

BS 3705   Recommendations for provision of space for domestic kitchen equipment

BS 3728   Specification for size designation of children's and infant's wear

BS 5304   Code of practice for safety of machinery

BS 4981   Specification for Mondopoint footwear sizing and marking system

BS 5511   Size designation of clothes − definitions and body measurement procedure

BS 5592   Size designation of clothes − headwear

BS 5873   Educational furniture

BS 5940   Office furniture

BS 6222   Domestic kitchen equipment

BS 6750   Specification for modular co-ordination in buildings

List of Tables